Twayne's English Authors Series

Sylvia E. Bowman, *Editor*

INDIANA UNIVERSITY

Lennox Robinson

 9

Lennox Robinson

By MICHAEL J. O'NEILL

University of Ottawa, Canada

Twayne Publishers, Inc.   ::   New York

To
Delia

Preface

Among the special gifts of the Anglo-Irish literary tradition to English literature are clarity, splendid wit, gaiety, and a sharply realistic approach to life. Descended from Protestant Anglo-Irish stock, Esmé Stuart Lennox Robinson, commonly known as Lennox Robinson, shared many of the characteristic traits of the writers in this tradition which went back to Swift and which reached through Goldsmith and Sheridan down to the most intellectual of modern Irish playwrights, Denis Johnston.

Lennox Robinson's contributions to the realms of literature during his long life-span of seventy-two years were many and varied. Besides being very productive in the theatre, he wrote a slender autobiographical novel, two autobiographies, and two biographies. In addition, he brought out collections of his essays and short stories, edited letters and memoirs, compiled several anthologies of Irish poetry, prepared an official history of the Abbey Theatre, and served briefly as a journalist and as a London drama critic. But his reputation today rests almost entirely upon his devoted work for the Abbey Theatre; consequently, it seems fitting that *Lennox Robinson* concern itself mainly with him as a "man of the theatre."

He began writing for the Irish theatre when Synge, its first great dramatist, was nearing his premature death. The production of Robinson's second play, *Cross Roads* (1909), at the Abbey Theatre was, in fact, postponed as a mark of respect for the burial of his famous predecessor. With the departure of Synge, a door closed on an era in which the poetic interpreters of the life of the folk were in the ascendant.

Lennox Robinson's arrival, however, coincided with the opening of another door through which were already entering in quick succession a different breed of Irish playwrights. They were almost ruthlessly interested in baring the harsher aspects, the sterner realities of Irish life. Robinson came at a time when the Abbey Theatre, as its poor attendance indicated, had not yet lived down the rancorous emotions provoked by Synge's *The Playboy of the Western World* (1907) among the then politically sensitive Irish. But the relevance of the dramatic material of Robinson and of his fellow realists to the changing Irish scene helped to promote the interest of the people in the Abbey and to shape it as a truly national theatre. Appropriately enough, also, this flowering of the Abbey as a national symbol formed an integral part of Ireland's emergence as a free nation after centuries of English rule.

1910 was a fateful year for Robinson, for Yeats, easily the most important, the most potent influence working upon his career, chose him at the early age of twenty-three to participate in molding the future destiny of the Abbey. Yeats, of course, had aspired at the outset to fashion a poetic theatre, but now he allowed Robinson to follow his own bent. And Robinson almost instinctively felt that "realism" would become the dominant mode. Under his auspices as manager, producer, and director—with only occasional demurrers from Yeats and Lady Gregory—the realistic folk play eventually established itself as the typical Abbey play.

Yeats, moreover, saw considerable promise in the dramas of Robinson's youth. After watching *Harvest* (1910) in performance, Yeats praised his protégé for "his serious intellect" and prophesied that he would "grow to be a great dramatist." Yeats's estimate was undoubtedly affected by his propensity to extol, even to overpraise, his friends and associates. Yet, if Robinson did not have the genius of Synge and O'Casey and did not achieve their international renown, he evolved, nevertheless, into an excellent playwright in the Abbey tradition.

From Robinson's pen for well over forty years flowed a steady stream of technically skilled plays, versatile in subject matter and urbane in the treatment of it. His comedies of Irish small-town life, especially, were always certain to please not only Abbey audiences but those throughout the English-speaking world. Concerning Robinson's greatest comic success, *The Whiteheaded Boy*, staged in 1916, one can readily agree with the verdict of Denis Johnston: "It will always be a classic prototype of the kind of play the Abbey did well during the first decades of its history."[1]

Prompting Robinson ever since he was old enough to have a mind and judgment of his own was a rather subtle and profound influence which he called "that strange Irish thing." Although he never explained its nature, "that strange Irish thing" would seem to be a unique fusion of an artist's idealism, catholicity of tastes, and love of country. One can observe it in action, for example, in his efforts to spread his love of beauty and of the theatrical arts to every corner of Ireland.

Still, there was nothing parochial about the "Irish thing," for Robinson also aspired to bring his country's tastes into the broad stream of the cultural life of Europe and America. Indeed, during a crucial exploratory period of his life, chiefly in the 1920's, his cosmopolitan interests grew sufficiently alluring to make him close his ears to the call of the nurturing "Irish thing." This new bent in his career as a writer led to a series of plays that reflected no special country, imitated the fashionable modes in the theatre during that period, and mirrored little or nothing of his own individual personality. His efforts to break away from the Abbey mold, nonetheless, had the beneficial effect of stimulating his fellow Irish dramatists to concern themselves with modern psychological problems.

But this "Irish thing," propitiously for him, refused to stay dormant for long; it once again exerted its sway and inspired him to seek anew for fresh material in Ireland. It guided him to the lives of the landed Anglo-Irish gentry whose decline he viewed with nostalgia and regret. More important still, it enabled him to find what was his best métier: gay, genial, and witty plays about the amusing aspects of small-town life in Ireland. These enhanced his reputation as a playwright. They also were the main source of whatever little income he derived from his writing. But one must remember that the smallness of Ireland's population and the consequent small audiences make it next to impossible for an Irish playwright who appeals principally to his fellow countrymen to live solely from what he earns by his pen.

Robinson's early dramas manifest his youthful desire to teach and to guide; by these means he hoped to improve the social, economic, and political conditions of the Irish people. Evident in these plays, too, is the mood of a disenchanted young idealist and romantic who is disquieted, frustrated, embittered by the gulf separating dream and fact. But as he grew older, his plays—

happily for his audiences and for himself—acquired more gentle, and more understanding attributes. Thus they became less didactic and less strained.

Though his early harshness was replaced with a kindly tolerence, his sense of disillusionment continued to erupt, sometimes even unexpectedly, in his later work. Interestingly enough, villains do not exist in his plays. Very many of his heroes, on the other hand, bring about their own downfall because their idealism thwarts them in their attempts to reconcile the real with the ideal.

Yet illusions can be both beautiful and foolish. So the pessimism of Robinson's disenchantment with the world about him—"his tendency to gloom" as Lady Gregory termed it—was his own favorite illusion. Like his idol Yeats, for artistic ends Robinson felt the need to wear a mask. But Robinson's mask served to disguise the fact that he was more hopeful about life and people than he wished to acknowledge.

MICHAEL J. O'NEILL

University of Ottawa
January, 1964

Acknowledgments

I am much indebted to all those whose help I have received while writing this book. At the outset, I wish to express my special thanks to Mrs. Lennox Robinson for her kindness and courtesy in making various manuscripts and valuable information available to me.

I am particularly indebted to the many people who have very generously contributed personal reminiscences of Lennox Robinson or who have very obligingly allowed me to consult material about him. Among these, I wish to acknowledge the assistance of Norris Davidson, Denis Johnston, Mrs. Brigid Ganly, Gerard Fay, Hilton Edwards, Shelah Richards, Walter Starkie, Mrs. Iris Wise, Teresa Deevy, Geraldine Cummins, Curtis Canfield, Monk Gibbon, Sean Dorman, Rutherford Mayne, Elizabeth Coxhead, Sean O'Casey, Daniel Corkery, Harold G. Merriam, Emerson Shuck, the Reverend George Hobson, Gerald Heard, Marc Connelly, W. Bridges-Adams, Ernest Blythe, Lady Longford, and *The Irish Times.*

Thanks are due to Dr. Hayes, Alf MacLochlainn, and the staff of the National Library of Ireland for their always courteous cooperation. Particular recognition goes to Mrs. Maureen O'Brien for her patience in typing a difficult manuscript.

I am also grateful to Curtis Brown, the literary agent of Lennox Robinson; to the Public Trustee and the Society of Authors for use of the letters from G. B. Shaw to Robinson; and to J. C. Medley for the letter from George Moore.

The quotations I have used from the works of Lennox Robinson are "granted by permission of the Estate of Lennox Robinson." For these rights I am most grateful. I also wish to record my indebtedness for being allowed to quote from the works of the following publishers:

Talbot Press, Dublin, that has also assumed the rights of Maunsel and Co., for *The Clancy Name, The Cross Roads, Harvest, The Dreamers, Patriots, Portrait, The White Blackbird,* and *The Whiteheaded Boy.*

To Macmillan, London, for *Is Life Worth Living?* (*Drama at Inish*), *The Big House, Killycreggs at Twilight, Church Street, Give a Dog, All's Over, Then?, Ever the Twain,* and *Bird's Nest.*

To Putnam, London, for *The Round Table* and *Lady Gregory's Journals.*

To Michael Joseph, London, for *Three Homes* and *Curtain Up.*

In a variety of ways the following have graciously given me their assistance, and to them I offer my cordial thanks: Dr. Brendan O'Brien, William P. Halstead, Harriet Cohen, Mrs. B. Clapp, J. J. Hogan, Roger McHugh, H. O. White, Margaret F. Reidy, Ignatius Lyons, Hubert Butler, Mrs. G. B. Kimberley, Dr. F. Lee Miesle, Mary Manning, Gordon Craig, Dr. Firmin H. Brown, Jr., Thomas McGreevy, T. R. Henn, Irene Collins, Mrs. Nancy Bizot, Dr. T. M. Sheehan, Helen W. Williard, Curator, the Theatre Collection, Harvard College.

Contents

Chronology

1886   Esmé Stuart Lennox Robinson born in Douglas, near Cork, on October 4; youngest son of seven children of Andrew Craig and Emily Jones Robinson.

1892   Robinson's father, formerly a stockbroker, becomes a minister of the Church of Ireland; the family moves to his parish in Kinsale, County Cork.

1900   In July the Robinsons are transferred to Ballymoney in West Cork. Lennox Robinson attends Bandon Grammar School after several years of private instruction.

1904   Formal education ends. Poor health caused irregular attendance at school.

1905– Years of "forced leisure" and ominivorous reading. Edits
1906   and publishes family magazine, *Contributions*.

1907   In August, at the Cork Opera House, is patriotically stirred by the Abbey Company's acting of Yeats's *Kathleen ni Houlihan* and *The Hour Glass* and of Lady Gregory's *Rising of the Moon*. Also in August, his first work, a poem, is printed in *The Royal Magazine*.

1908   October 8, at the Abbey Theatre, Robinson sees acted the first production of his first play, *The Clancy Name, a Tragedy in One Act*. A revised version was produced on September 30, 1909, and published in *Two Plays* by Maunsel and Co. Ltd., Dublin, in 1911.

1909   April 1, at the Abbey, first production of *The Cross Roads, a Play in a Prologue and Two Acts*. The revised version on February 3, 1910, omitted the prologue. Maunsel, Dublin, published the original version in 1909. The Cork Dramatic Society at the Dun Theatre, Cork, first presents Robinson's *The Lesson of His Life, a Comedy in One Act* on December 2. Near the end of 1909, Yeats and Lady Gregory appoint Robinson producer (director of plays) and manager of the Abbey Theatre. Leaves County Cork for Dublin.

1910   January to March, in London, as Shaw's nominal secretary, learning the arts of the theatre from Shaw, Granville Barker, and Boucicault. Returns in March to the Abbey to direct his first play as producer. Remains as manager and producer until the first week in June, 1914. Stages his *Harvest, a Play in Three Acts*, at the Abbey on May 19; published by Maunsel, Dublin, in 1911, with the revised version of *The Clancy Name* in *Two Plays*.

1911   Becomes a member of the Arts Club, a center for many of Dublin's literati and artists. Manages the July tour of the Abbey Company in England. Leaves in September with Yeats for the first American tour of the Company.

1912   Returns from the United States to direct his *Patriots, a Play in Three Acts*, opening at the Abbey on April 11. Maunsel publishes it. From June 20 to July 4, directs Irish plays in London at the Royal Court Theatre.

1913   Goes to America with Lady Gregory for the third tour of the Company after remaining behind in Dublin for the second one of the previous year. Lady Gregory's criticism of his management of the tour leads to his leaving the Abbey in June 1914.

1914   Invited to London to direct an Irish play at the Royal Court Theatre in June. Afterwards makes the first of almost annual trips to the Continent. Returns to Cork and joins Redmond's Irish Volunteers to fight for the Allies.

1915   A temporary employee of the government at Dublin Castle. February 10, at the Abbey, the first production of his *The Dreamers, a Play in Three Acts;* published in the same year by Maunsel. During the summer Sir Horace Plunkett assigns Robinson to Kerry and Limerick as Organizing Librarian for the Carnegie United Kingdom Trust; stays with the Trust until December, 1924.

1916   On December 13, within eight months of the Easter Rising in Dublin, the Abbey presents the most successful of all Robinson's plays, *The Whiteheaded Boy, a Comedy in Three Acts*. Putnam & Company, Ltd., London, issued it in 1921. Three other editions of it were printed between 1921 and 1955.

1917 Maunsel publishes his only novel, the autobiographical *A Young Man From the South.*

1918 His *The Lost Leader, a Play in Three Acts,* is produced on February 19 at the Abbey, and published by the Eigeas Press, Ltd., Dublin. The Talbot Press issues a collection of four political sketches called *Dark Days.* With Yeats, James Stephens, and Ernest Boyd, Robinson sponsors the Drama League (1919-28) to encourage the international theatre in Ireland. Later directs and acts in plays for the League. Active in promoting the Irish Playwrights' Association for protecting the interests of dramatists.

1919 Yeats and Lady Gregory recall him in April to be manager and producer of the Abbey.

1920– Contributed stories and articles to English, American, and
1953   Irish magazines: these included the *Athenaeum, New Statesman and Nation, London Mercury, Spectator, The Dial, The Irish Statesman, Ireland Today, The Bell,* and *Irish Harvest. The Best British Short Stories of 1927* included his "Quest." Talbot Press, Dublin, in 1920 publishes his *Eight Short Stories,* written between 1912 and 1919. Edits *Further Letters of John B. Yeats* for the Churchtown Press, Dublin, in 1920 as a sequel to Pound's previous edition of the letters of Yeats's father.

1921 Father dies at seventy-nine on December 31, at Ballymoney, County Cork.

1922 On January 31, three weeks after the ratification of the Anglo-Irish Treaty, Robinson presents his *The Round Table, a Comic Tragedy in Three Acts* at the Abbey. This was published by Putnam & Company, Ltd., London, in 1924. The revised version, classified as *A Comedy,* was acted at The Playhouse Theatre, Liverpool, on March 16, 1927, and published in London by Macmillan & Company, Ltd., in 1928. During the Irish Civil War he produces his *Crabbed Youth and Age, a Little Comedy,* at the Abbey on November 14. First published in *Theatre Arts Monthly* in January, 1924; Putnam & Company, Ltd., London, also brought it out in 1924.

1923 The Abbey Board of Directors appoints him fellow director; remains a director until the end of his life.

1924 Joins *The Observer,* London, in January as a writer of the weekly drama column, "At the Play," replacing St. J. Ervine; continues as newspaper critic until August, 1925. On February 19, produces his *Never the Time and the Place, a Little Comedy in One Act* at the Abbey and publishes it in *The Dublin Magazine* for May; printed also by Carter, Belfast, in 1953.

1925   Moves from a house on the estate of Sir Horace Plunkett, in Foxrock, County Dublin, to "Sorrento" in Dalkey, south of Dublin, on the sea coast. On March 31, at the Abbey, he stages his *Portrait, a Play in Two Sittings;* also produces at the Abbey his *The White Blackbird, a Play in Three Acts,* on October 12. Both plays were published in 1926 by the Talbot Press, Dublin. Opens the Peacock Theatre as an experimental adjunct to the Abbey in November. Edits *A Golden Treasury of Irish Verse* for Macmillan, London.

1926   Establishes the Abbey School of Acting at the Peacock. Stages on September 6 at the Abbey his *The Big House, Four Scenes in its Life.* Published by Macmillan, London, in 1928.

1927   Edits *Poems by Thomas Parnell* for the Cuala Press, Dublin.

1928   With Yeats he helps Ninette de Valois to open a School of Ballet at the Peacock. October 22, the Abbey presents his very successful *The Far-Off Hills, a Comedy in Three Acts,* published in 1931 by Chatto and Windus, Ltd., London. Edits *A Little Anthology of Modern Irish Verse* for the Cuala Press. Spends October, 1928, through January, 1929, in the United States on a lecture tour between New York and Chicago; directs his *The Whiteheaded Boy* at the Civic Theatre, Detroit, in November.

1929   At the Strand Theatre, London, on January 20, his *Give a Dog, a Play in Three Acts,* is first presented; in 1928, Macmillan, London, published it in a Collected Edition of his plays, entitled *Plays.* Marking his twenty-first anniversary as a playwright, he produces his *Ever the Twain, a Comedy in Three Acts,* on October 8, at the Abbey. Macmillan, London, published it in 1930.

1930   In the spring, visits the United States as guest producer (director) and lecturer at Amherst College, Carnegie Institute of Technology, and the University of Michigan. Teaches and directs at the Summer School of the University of Montana.

1931 Modernizes Sheridan's *The Critic*, which he presents at the Abbey on January 6. Marries Dorothy Travers Smith, granddaughter of Professor Edward Dowden, in London on September 8. Goes to the United States and Canada as advance lecturer for the Abbey Company during its extensive North American tour of twenty-six states, beginning in October, 1931. Returns prior to the death of Lady Gregory in May, 1932. Constable, Ltd., London, prints his *Bryan Cooper*, a biography of an Anglo-Irish landlord.

1932 On July 25, at the Abbey, produces his *All's Over, Then?, a Play in Three Acts;* published by Macmillan, London, in 1935. Mother dies, aged eighty-two. Chosen as one of the original Academicians of the Irish Academy of Letters on September 18.

1933 Stages his *Drama at Inish, an Exaggeration in Three Acts* at the Abbey on February 6. This was renamed *Is Life Worth Living?* for its first London production in 1934; was published under its double title by Macmillan, London, in 1933. Assistant Director at Elstree, London, for film *General John Regan*.

1934 Produces his *Church Street, a Play in One Act* at the Abbey on May 21. Macmillan, London, published it in 1935. Joins the Abbey Company on its American tour sometime between October, 1934, and June, 1935.

1936 At the Gate Theatre, Dublin, on August 18, Hilton Edwards produces Robinson's *When Lovely Woman, a Comedy in Three Acts*.

1937 The Abbey presents his *Killycreggs in Twilight, a Play in Three Acts*. Macmillan, London, published it in 1939.

1938 Michael Joseph, Ltd., London, issues *Three Homes*, an autobiography that Robinson wrote with the aid of his sister and brother. Organizes the Abbey Theatre Festival in August at which he lectures on Lady Gregory. The Abbey stages his *Bird's Nest, a Play in Three Acts* on September 12; published by Macmillan, London, in 1939 with *Killycreggs in Twilight*.

1939 Edits for Macmillan, London, *The Irish Theatre*, containing the lectures delivered at the Abbey Theatre Festival. Yeats dies.

1940   Writes on Yeats as a person and as a dramatist in *Scattering Branches* (a collection of tributes to Yeats); published by Macmillan, London. Makes adaptation of Maupassant's *Boule de Suif* as *Roly Poly;* directed by Hilton Edwards at the Gate Theatre on November 19. December 25, Radio Eireann broadcasts Robinson's brief comedy, *Let Well Alone;* published in *The Bell* for January, 1941.

1941   Directs his *Forget Me Not, a Play in Three Acts* at the Abbey on December 26.

1942   Michael Joseph, London, prints Robinson's autobiography, *Curtain Up.*

1945   His *Towards an Appreciation of the Theatre* issued by Metropolitan Publishing Company, Ltd., Dublin.

1946   Edits *Lady Gregory's Journals* for Putnam & Company, Ltd., London.

1947   At the *Sign of the Three Candles Press,* Dublin, publishes his *Pictures in a Theatre, A Conversation Piece.* Visiting professor of English and Speech for the fall term at Bowling Green State University, Bowling Green, Ohio. Founding member of the Actors' Church Union.

1948   The University Theatre of Bowling Green State University stages the first production of his *The Lucky Finger, a Comedy in Three Acts* on January 19. A revised version was presented at the Abbey on August 23, 1948, and published by Samuel French, New York, in 1949. Trinity College, Dublin, awards him an honorary Doctor of Literature. Brown and Nolan, Ltd., Dublin, brings out *Palette and Plough,* a biography of his friend, Dermod O'Brien.

1949   The Directors of the Abbey commission him to write a history of the Abbey; published in London as *Ireland's Abbey Theatre* by Sidgwick and Jackson, Ltd., December, 1951.

1950   Directs his *The Whiteheaded Boy* at the Edinburgh Festival.

1951   Irish representative at the UNESCO Congress for the International Theatre Institute at Oslo in May. After his return, when the Abbey burned on July 17, agrees with his fellow directors to keep the Abbey going at the Queens Theatre.

1952   Suffers his first attack of angina. Writes preface for Geraldine Cummins's *Dr. E. OE. Somerville,* published by Dakers, London.

1953   Appointed honorary patron of the All-Ireland Drama Council for the promotion of Amateur Drama Festivals at which he frequently adjudicated up to his death. Writes a weekly column, "I Sometimes Think" for the daily *Irish Press* until 1956. Talbot Press published a selection of these columns under the same title in 1956.

1954   Edwards produces Robinson's *The Demon Lover, a Play in Three Acts* on June 21 at the Gaiety Theatre. Robinson directs Yeats's *On Baile's Strand* at the Queens Theatre to commemorate the fiftieth anniversary of the Abbey.

1956   In May, makes two recordings for Spoken Arts, New York: "Plays and Memories of W. B. Yeats," and "Poems and Memories of W. B. Yeats." The government of Communist China invites Robinson, as senior Irish dramatist, to China to lecture on Shaw for the centenary celebration of Shaw's birth. Elected Chairman of P.E.N. for Ireland.

1958   His broadcast for the British Broadcasting Corporation to honor the centenary of the Irish novelist, Dr. Edith Somerville, is published as "Queen of West Carberry" in *The Listener,* May 22. With Donagh McDonagh, edits *The Oxford Book of Irish Verse* for the Oxford University Press. October 14, dies of heart failure; buried not far from the tomb of Dean Swift in St. Patrick's Cathedral, Dublin.

Lennox Robinson

CHAPTER 1

The Making of a Nationalist

I

LENNOX ROBINSON, who died of heart failure on October 14, 1958, at the Glensilva Nursing Home close to his private residence in Monkstown, County Dublin, was among the leading figures of the now famous Irish Literary Movement. Through the versatility of his contributions to the Irish theatre as a playwright, manager, producer,* director, critic, historian, and actor, he gained recognition as Ireland's most complete "Man of the Theatre." His prestige, however, never dulled his sincere sense of modesty. He would be the first to point out that good fortune brought him into his country's literary rebirth at its most fruitful moments when W. B. Yeats, Lady Gregory, George Moore, Edward Martyn, and J. M. Synge were valiantly and splendidly shaping fresh literary ideals and striving to give new life to the moribund theatrical values in England and Ireland at the turn of the twentieth century.

An ingrained shyness remained to haunt Robinson nearly all of his life, and this characteristic caused some to consider him either regrettably supercilious or irritatingly aloof. Yet, he tried to overcome his shyness because he was very fond of people and of their company. In truth, his gregarious inclinations fulfilled an intense inner urge and, at the same time, helped him to become engrossed in the source of most of his dramatic material—Irish life. So he came to be a responsive and discerning observer of the Irish scene, agreeably absorbed by its endemic surprises, incongruities, gaiety, and sadness.

In the life of Ireland he was also one of its most familiar personalities. Even remote villages knew him from his visits while judging the acting and directing at their drama festivals. No com-

* In Great Britain and Ireland the functions of the producer correspond to those of the director in the United States, and vice versa.

munity was too small for him, no journey too long, no hours too late if by his presence he could thereby spread interest in the drama among the people. Yeats's vision was also his. Wherever Robinson went, his mincing gait, his lean, emaciated, hatless but well-mufflered figure made him easily recognizable as he sauntered along apparently caught up in his own private world. Or, as one of his friends quipped about him, "Lennox seems ever alone and palely loitering."

Yet his vague unworldly air, his fragile, slender appearance, and his weary plaintive voice could be rather deceptive. He had the courage of a lion when fighting for his convictions, and he firmly defended any cause he felt strongly about. Throughout his life, moreover, he never seemed to have lost an instinctive shrewdness tempered by his humaneness; as a result, he could be quite practical when managing the affairs of the Abbey Theatre.

At his beloved Abbey he was fondly known to at least four decades of theatregoers. There, one could often see him wandering restlessly between its foyer and back-stage, giving instructions to his appreciative box-office and program attendants, or offering last-minute encouragement to the actors nervous and alert for their cues. There, too, one could watch him almost magically winding and unwinding his long legs as he squirmed in his seat while chatting with some famous visitor to the theatre or exchanging critical opinions with Yeats and Lady Gregory. That first-rate novelist of Irish provincial middle-class life, Kate O'Brien, who became Robinson's friend later in her life, offers perceptive glimpses of him during her student days in Dublin. At that time, between 1917 and 1919, his plays were beginning to win fame for him at the Abbey during its heyday. Regularly in attendance there, Kate O'Brien became much impressed by this "strange elongated boyish man" who, upon his return as manager in 1919, came out before the curtains to make announcements or even to request better manners from the audience. To her, as he stood in the glare of the spotlight peering myopically through his old-fashioned, wire-rimmed glasses, he seemed "hesitant always, his long hands twisted about a long white scarf, his eyes half closed, his voice fluting past us to the ceiling. But he always said what he desired to say, and always commanding attention."[1]

The affection with which he was held by Dubliners can be gauged by the many whimsical stories told about him. Some of these, in fact, he even delighted in telling against himself. Probably the most popular one deals with his tenderness for animals and the more delicate things of nature. Once when he was on the upper level of a double-decker bus en route to his home in County Dublin, he lurched precariously down the aisle of the jolting vehicle and opened a window to allow an imprisoned butterfly to escape. Later, the playwright's companion queried why he had gone to all that bother. Robinson gently explained: "I'm told butterflies only live for 24 hours, and if you had only that short time left, imagine having to live it on top of a Dalkey bus."

On the other hand, with his fellow man he could on occasion lapse into tactlessness, being fond of the light, barbed thrust or the maliciously witty phrase. But the tartness was most often mitigated by humor, and the victim rarely considered the personal injury as cruel. The noted Dublin director, Hilton Edwards, for instance, recalls one experience involving his equally famous partner, Micheál MacLiammoir: "Lennox had invited MacLiammoir to act the leading male role in his *Ever the Twain* at the Abbey. When he, in turn, questioned Lennox what he should wear in the play, he replied, 'Oh anything! You know I describe the character you will play as that d-r-e-a-d-f-u-l young man in the d-r-e-a-d-f-u-l tweeds. The suit you have on will do splendidly.'" Edwards, however, good-humoredly and urbanely adds, "To do Lennox justice the suit that MacLiammoir was wearing— we were both very penurious then—certainly fitted the bill."[2]

II

In Douglas, now a suburb of southeast Cork, Lennox Robinson was born on October 4, 1886, the youngest of seven children. Douglas was then a village of woolen mills, terraces, and the small dwellings of workers. His parents had moved there the previous year to a commodious, pleasantly rambling country house named "Westgrove," near the crest of a hill behind the village. Three miles away to the northward could be seen the spires of the city of Cork.

The same year that Lennox Robinson was born, Gladstone's first bill to resolve the live issue of "Home Rule" for Ireland was defeated in the English parliament, and W. B. Yeats was just beginning to publish his first poems. Further, during the first decade of Robinson's life occurred a series of events having important bearing upon Ireland's future political and cultural life. Three of the most significant of these happened within the brief span of three years. In 1891, Parnell died, leaving the country in deep mourning at the loss of his brilliant leadership; in 1892, Yeats promoted the founding of the Irish National Literary Society at Dublin; and in 1893, Douglas Hyde organized the nonpolitical Gaelic League to preserve and revive the Irish language and culture.

Lennox Robinson's family came from the staunchly Protestant, Anglo-Irish class which had been dominant in Ireland for very many generations. Having lived in Ireland that long, they considered themselves Irish; but, chiefly because of their religion, they were slightly *déraciné* in the minds of their fellow Catholic-Irish. Yet, as Robinson asserted, they belonged to no other country in the world—certainly not to England.

At baptism, his ancestry-conscious parents gave Robinson the highly romantic names of Esmé, Stuart, and Lennox. And not surprisingly they had difficulty in deciding which of these to call him. They dropped the first one early in his life and finally settled on Stuart. Only after he had been several years a playwright did he begin to use the name by which he is commonly known throughout the literary world. Yeats, upon designating Robinson as manager and director of the Abbey, considered that the initials S.L., then used by Robinson, were devoid of any personality. Why not use instead, suggested Yeats, the more distinguished, the more dramatic sounding Lennox.

His father, Andrew Craig Robinson, was secretly proud of the lineage of his own family and of that of his wife Emily. He could trace his ancestral line back to Esmé Stuart, Earl of Lennox, the notorious relative of Darnley; she could trace hers back to Wales, for her father, a Dublin solicitor named Jones, maintained that he was a descendant of Owen Glendower. Later in his life, Robinson recalled that before he was twelve his father painstakingly showed him the long family tree and all their distinguished connections. Then, as his father was solemnly rolling up the parchment, he remarked, "I have shown you this to let you know what you are sprung from, but you must remember that no gentleman ever boasts of his birth." [3]

Robinson's father, a gentle other-worldly person to whom the abstract appealed little, had studied law at Trinity College, Dublin, while Mahaffy, Dowden, and Lecky were there; but he had never practiced. In 1892, at the age of fifty, he decided to satisfy a long and fondly cherished ambition by becoming a minister of the Church of Ireland. The acceptance of this late call to the clerical life meant that he had to abandon his occupation as a stockbroker in Cork and with it a comfortable living. His religious vocation now compelled him to depend instead upon the proportionately small income of £150 to support and rear his large family. His action, just the same, was not unpremeditated— was not one that lightly jeopardized the future of his family by throwing aside his sound business. For all his life, his father, as Robinson explained, "had taken a leading part in Church affairs. In fact, there were few departments of Church life in which he had not done more than one man's share." [4]

His income as a clergyman forced Andrew Robinson into hard ways the rest of his life to bring up his family in a manner called for by his standing in the community. Only by selling off his small investments, little by little, did he manage to exist and to educate his children. But he was endowed with an innately optimistic nature and always looked to the future for the solution of his difficulties. At heart Andrew Robinson, as his son pointed out, "was a gambler, perhaps he was too long at stockbroking and it was in his blood." [5]

Robinson apparently inherited more of his father's characteristics than his mother's. If his mother could be almost sentimentally fond of elegance, she could also be strong and masterful. His father, on the other hand, was a delightfully whimsical person with a fanciful turn of mind. What is more, he had considerable sympathetic insights into people's feelings; and he offered them his warm support when needed.

The playwright's grandmother lived near the family and her firm and forceful personality left a lasting impression upon him. The intensity of her Protestant faith made her completely scorn the beliefs held by Catholics, whom she regarded as damned beyond hope of redemption. Yet neither her religious dogmatism nor her sternness impressed the family as much as her deep regard for strict truth which she tried at all times to imprint on their receptive minds.

When the author was six years old, his father received his first assignment—to a curacy in the British garrison town of Kinsale, about twenty miles south-west of Douglas on the Cork coast. This move quite upset the even tenor of the family's ways. It meant a considerable falling off in their living standards when compared with their pleasant experiences at "Westgrove." Society in this very historic Cork town—with its long memories of ancient deeds of daring and battle, with its current awareness of the frequent coming and going of British regiments—was strongly Protestant, Unionist, and anti-national. Into this conservative and loyalist mold Robinson's parents easily fitted, and he himself never forgot the impression this milieu left upon his young mind.

On one occasion he went with his mother to a "Watch Night" service to commemorate the last day of 1897. Filled with gloomy forebodings because the coming year would mark the anniversary of 1798, his mother exclaimed, "God grant that those dreadful Nationalists will not attempt an insurrection of some sort!" Young Robinson then vaguely "felt that the Nationalists didn't believe in England and were consequently dangerous and not to be associated with, just as Catholics didn't believe in the true Protestant God." [6]

As a young boy, Robinson was not robust; he was thin and lanky and his solemn face was capped by light brown hair. His ill-health worried his mother, causing her to make him her pet, her "Whiteheaded Boy." Consequently, much to his boyish disgust, she continued to keep him dressed in a black velvet suit with a lace collar for a much longer period than he wished. Because he was the youngest and weakest member of the family, his brothers would not allow him to participate in their robust games and activities.

This rebuff first threw him back upon the friendship of his sister and her friends, only to find that they talked about matters he did not understand. So he was left without friends of his own age. But, as he went on to explain, "perhaps I might have had, for I remember one of my Mother's favorite sayings to me was, 'A great man that has friends must show himself friendly.' I did not show myself friendly, I was peevish and tiresome, I was sentimental, I was also quite an accomplished little liar." [7]

He found himself, time and again, being confined to the companionship of his mother and older people. But this seeming disadvantage turned out later in his life to have been an advantage. It helped, for example, to put him on easy terms with intelligent, capable, and dedicated older women such as Sara Purser and Lady Gregory. It also assisted him as a writer; for, as he pointed out, "one of the few things I could do well was to write the thoughts of middle-aged, ordinary people. I am sure that this is because I had no friends of my own age, my closest companions were old maids." [8]

To give variety to his experiences, as a youth he turned to the solitary imaginative pleasures of nature. These were easily accessible to him as he strolled by himself through the countryside surrounding his home. There he found much to admire and thus satisfy and ripen his romantic inclinations—green-arched, winding lanes; fields yellow with cowslips or buttercups; shower-sparkling trees; and lazy streams groping through shadowy woods.

This withdrawal within himself for his own diversion made him an agonizingly shy and very introspective young boy. So self-conscious did he become that whenever he was invited to parties, his usual means of excusing himself was to develop a headache by hitting his head against the wall of his bedroom. His shyness, though, did not prevent his innate dramatic instincts from coming to the fore. As a matter of fact, on occasion he liked to show off a small talent for recitation by declaiming for church audiences in Kinsale's Fisherman's Hall where his father regularly held prayer meetings. His favorite piece, which he illustrated with lantern slides, was "Curfew Shall Not Ring Tonight."

Since Robinson's father was a clergyman, religion, of course, played a dominant role in the daily life of the entire household. Sunday especially was crowded with religious activities, and little time was left for much else in young Robinson's life. These activities began, he recalled, with "early Communion for those who could attend, morning service at half-past eleven, this being our High Mass of the day, with the soldiers marching to it headed by their band . . . and a three-quarters of an hour sermon by the Rector. Home then to a quick dinner and at three o'clock to Sunday-School in the Fisherman's Hall." [9]

The family was not allowed to play games on Sunday, but anyone could read for an hour or more during the late afternoon before teatime. Their reading was censored but not severely; the romances of Charlotte Yonge and Louisa May Alcott, for example, were acceptable "Sunday-books." The busy day ended with evening church and this, in turn, during certain seasons, was followed by a prayer meeting or by hymn singing in the Fisherman's Hall. In particular, the religious fervor of the visiting Manx and Cornish fishermen as they sang the hymn "What will you do at the swelling of the Jordan" lingered long in Robinson's memories of his youth.

Because Kinsale had no school to which one of his age could be sent and because Cork was thought too far for a weak boy to travel to school, Robinson received a rudimentary education at home. First, he studied with the family governess and later with his mother, his sister, and his father. Upon completing his home schooling, the family considered him fit to try for the preparatory grade in the Intermediate Examination. However, he became sick with scarlatina and accordingly did not pass this examination. A year later he again took the same test and again failed. Disarmingly he once admitted: "Perhaps I should not make illness an excuse. The only examinations I ever passed were scripture ones; in them I seldom got less than 90 per cent and on several occasions the full hundred." [10]

After seven unsatisfactory years in Kinsale, Robinson's father in July, 1900, was appointed rector of the West-Cork parish of Ballymoney lying in the peaceful valley of the river Bandon. This advancement allowed the family to leave behind them their unpleasant thoughts of Kinsale and to return to a life somewhat similar to the one they had spent at "Westgrove." The new home had a walled garden, fruit trees, thirty acres of land for tillage, and pasture for sheep and pigs. Attached to the property also were extensive stables, where in those days, before the coming of the automobile, church-going farmers could shelter their horses and carriages or place their bicycles.

The farmers in his father's new parish were financially comfortable; but their houses, although substantial looking on the exterior, were marked almost by squalor in the interior. Robinson's description of the background of their lives serves as a helpful introduction to the material from which he fashioned some of the more bitter plays of his earlier writing years:

They had no flower-gardens, perhaps a neglected rose-bush would grow beside the door—that door which could be only approached by skirting the midden . . . . and the interior of their house was as dismal as the exterior. The air was sweet and good and the land was rich, there should have been no need to stint in milk and butter and eggs—yet tuberculosis was rampant. There was little comfort, there was no graciousness in their lives, the balance in the bank must grow and if possible more land must be bought. Perhaps a son would be a priest—money would not be spared for that—and now and then an adventurous boy or girl would break from home and become a doctor or a nurse. Marriages were "made" marriages, a matter of acres and cattle and, as a rule, were contented unions.[11]

Robinson, nonetheless, also indicates that despite their disregard for the amenities of life, these farmers had wit and intelligence; if they were hard-fisted about big things, they were very generous about small ones.

Very shortly after the family had settled down in its new home, his parents sent him to the nearby Bandon Grammar School, founded in 1542 for Protestant students. At this historic institution he "learned with avidity but superficially, got splendid marks from day to day and had forgotten nearly everything when examination time came." [12] As might be expected, he was good at writing—so good that his description of a storm at sea, much to his chagrin, was suspected of being copied from a sea story for boys. Actually it was not, but the teacher, after hesitating between full marks and a caning for cheating, compromised by giving no marks.

He attended school for only a year, and again ill-health compelled him to interrupt his studies. He began to suffer from a succession of prostrating headaches; previously intermittent, now they were chronic. The family doctor diagnosed that young Robinson was growing too fast and that to avoid catching infection he would be better off resting at home to conserve his energy. On this account his formal schooling, except for a brief interlude at Bandon when he was seventeen, was brought to an end. The doctor's orders also led Robinson's parents to regard him as a convalescent. Hence they limited his lessons to one hour a day under the tutelage of his classically trained father who taught him Latin.

These years of forced leisure, which lasted until he was twenty, were far from being wasted. During that period he devoted his time "to music, to rough shooting, and fishing, to reading, to a little boyish writing." [13] Further, with the aid of his cousin and any willing member of his family he brought out and wrote pieces for a small private monthly magazine called *Contributions*. At first, many of his friends and other relations contributed to it, though later they fell away. Then both he and his cousin under a variety of pen names had to write for the magazine themselves.

While writing, to be sure, greatly appealed to him then, the love of music had also been in his veins ever since the age of seven when he began to take violin lessons. And for a space of time, during his early adolescence, the thoughts of some day becoming a professional musician had an even greater allure for him than the prospects of a career in the literary world. Willingly he made sacrifices for his musical interests, and, from the money earned from his bees and chickens during his "convalescence," he bought among other musical scores a complete set of Beethoven's piano sonatas.

As he grew older he showed some ability for harmony playing and composition, an ability that he sought to develop through correspondence lessons in harmony. But hampering him were the rather limited facilities at his disposal for advanced training. He grew discouraged, and gradually his dreams for a career in music faded away. Regretfully he realized that he could never be an outstanding composer, that he had quite limited talent, and that the best he could hope for was to be a third-rate organist in some small Irish town.[14]

Notwithstanding his severely critical appraisal of his deficiencies as a musician, he retained throughout his life a keen appreciation of music and of musical trends. He also included among his admiring friends such famous members of the musical world as Harriet Cohen and Sir Arnold Bax. In addition, he gained tremendous satisfaction when Yeats, distrusting the more elaborate techniques of contemporary composers, asked him in 1926 and 1927 to prepare the music for the choruses of *Oedipus Rex* and of *Oedipus at Colonus*. Moreover, Radio Eireann later broadcast one of the songs he had composed during his youth.

As compensation for the gaps in his education, Robinson intensified his reading in the books in the small family library which had for its nucleus nearly all of the first editions of Dickens. Allied to this, through his associations with a bookish clerical colleague of his father, he read Meredith, Hardy, and other modern novelists; he also borrowed such serious magazines as *The Cornhill, The Fortnightly,* and *The Nineteenth Century* from a lending library in Cork.

The limitations of Robinson's country environment, and the absence of a well-stocked library caused him to regret that he could not "idle" to better purpose; yet he also found some consolation in the fact that these leisurely "idling" days offered him many valuable experiences for his later career as a writer. In time they furnished him with the opportunity to scrutinize closely Irish country life, the life of the small farmer, and the life of the laborer.

Especially meaningful for him was the friendship he cultivated, as a young man, with the O'Neill-Daunts, a prosperous and cultured Catholic family living near Ballymoney in a nineteenth-century, Gothic-style castle. The O'Neill-Daunts greatly helped to alter his conservative political beliefs by introducing him to their nationalistic outlook acquired from their father who was at one time an active henchman of O'Connell. They had hundreds of back issues of *The Nation* newspaper, and these Robinson read avidly. Weaned away from the Unionist atmosphere of his home surroundings, he began for the first time to think seriously about Irish politics. Later, the O'Neill-Daunts encouraged him to widen his interests by providing him with histories of Ireland, Irish memoirs, and many other books about Irish affairs.

When he was almost twenty, he thought he might like to be a schoolteacher. Through a teachers' agency in London, he was offered the post of English and music teacher at a preparatory school in Wellington, Shropshire. But he held this position only for one term. Of this failure he said: "Since I knew nothing myself, I could not teach even preparatory boys." [15] Yet while at this school, a simple incident helped to intensify and give firmer direction to the growing spirit of nationalism that the O'Neill-Daunts had nourished in him. This happened in 1906 when the English newspapers reported the death of Michael Davitt, who once had suffered imprisonment in England as a Fenian:

Something scornful was said by one of the English masters about him, I don't think he was even dignified by being called a "rebel," he was just a disorderly Irishman who had been in gaol. It stirred my resentment . . . . a year or so later I was to see in a little shop in Ballineen,

Arthur Griffith's weekly paper *Sinn Fein* and buy it and subscribe later to his daily paper and buy Sinn Fein stamps to put on my letters, and to see one hot afternoon in the Cork Opera House a performance by the Abbey Theatre Company of *Kathleen ni Houlihan* and *The Rising of the Moon.*[16]

Robinson, by means of this brief historical survey, thus reviews the most important final steps in his political conversion from his earlier Unionist sympathies, inherited from his family and his environment, to his complete identification with the Irish nationalist cause. Of these experiences, easily the most vital was the permanent imprint left on his mind, heart, and imagination by Yeats's patriotic *Kathleen ni Houlihan*. His radical awakening not only made him a confirmed nationalist, but also opened wide the gates leading to his future career in the theatre. Less than two months afterwards, he began writing his first play.

CHAPTER 2

The Bitterness and
Didacticism of the Novice

I The Emergence of Realism

THE whole of modern Irish drama, as Dame Ellis-Fermor observed, is a seamless texture; the early poetic movement merges with the folk movement, and this, in turn, gradually coalesces with the realistic tradition.[1] If one examines this triple blending more closely in its earliest days, one can distinguish two essentially different phases: first, the heroic legend and poetic dramas of the folk encouraged by the founders of the Irish literary revival; and, second, in close sequence the emergence of the more successful and ultimately dominant realistic school furthered by their successors. Among those playwrights forming the vanguard of the second phase was Lennox Robinson.

In the beginning, Yeats easily held the ascendancy; he had as his aim a two-fold aspiration to put "our heroic age into verse" and "to bring upon the stage the deeper thoughts and emotions of Ireland" as a means of achieving "a return to the people." Not only did he bring together a band of devotees in Ireland who shared his beliefs on restoring poetry, ritualism, and austere simplicity to the theatre, but he also set a sterling example by writing plays exhibiting a fresh spirit of poetry.

While advancing the cause of the Irish drama, Yeats had a strong ally in his equally individualistic associate, Edward Martyn. Both writers thought that the decadent commercialism of the English theatre at the turn of the century prevented the creation of drama deserving of the name of art. Thus they were in accord at the outset when they joined with Lady Gregory to establish a National Literary Theatre in 1898: something should be done to offset the influence of the English stage. Looming large before them was the impact of the revolutionary work of Ibsen on the

Continent. So they easily agreed that Ibsen would be an admirable writer to imitate. But they differed over what aspect of Ibsen's dramas should be held up as a model for Irish dramatists to follow.

Martyn, somewhat ahead of his time, realized the need in Ireland for a social drama which would gather its general inspiration and subject matter from the life of the middle classes. Particularly in the social and psychological dramas of the Norwegian master he saw what he wanted for his guide and stimulus. Yet, not until later in the history of the Irish theatre, when the social and economic prestige of the middle classes increased in Ireland, did the validity and relevance of Martyn's theories become more fully recognized. Yeats, on the other hand, in the light of his solitary vision, could give his approval only to the romantic plays of Ibsen; the social dramas of Ibsen, he thought, were lacking in beautiful, vivid language.

Further, a fateful concurrence of events involving Yeats, the Fay brothers, and George Russell (A.E.) happened at that time which gave Yeats's hopes their chance to achieve a temporary and partial fulfillment and also helped to postpone the realization of Martyn's objectives. Poet and dreamer as he was, Yeats was realistic enough to see the need for folk plays, for plays rooted in the soil, to give fuller substance to Irish literature. By this accurate appraisal of Irish life he put himself in accord with one of its paramount realities: the important role of the countryman in the Irish picture.

Equally significant, too, was the relationship Yeats established by chance with the two Fays. Both were talented in the arts of the stage, and both also aspired to make the small Ormonde Dramatic Society, under their guidance, the nucleus of a national theatre for Ireland. Through the actors of this society they sought to cultivate a native tradition of acting, based chiefly on simplicity of style and the elimination of the "star" system.[2] In these objectives, the Fays showed themselves in basic accord with part of Yeats's program for reforming the theatre. Had he not asked that words be restored to their ancient sovereignty and that acting be simplified to allow concentration on the voice?

At the suggestion of George Russell, who had already given the Fays his *Deirdre* to act, Yeats came to one of the Ormonde Dramatic Society's rehearsals; and what he saw impressed him,

On very special occasions he had opportunities of getting to Dublin to enjoy the theatrical fare of the capital, and he looked forward to these visits with great anticipation. One of these trips he made in 1907, when the earnings from his bees provided him with enough money for a three-day excursion to Dublin. For his short stay there young Robinson had mapped out a schedule of theatregoing at the Gaiety and at the Royal intensive enough for the most ardent lover of the theatre:

He was going to see Mr. Beerbohm Tree in *The Red Lamp;* and the next evening he was going to see him again in *Colonel Newcome,* and on Wednesday he was going to the Gaiety Theatre to see Mr. Forbes Robertson and Miss Gertrude Eliott in *Mice and Men.* It was going to be an orgy. Three theatres in three days and such starry actors, such wonderful plays. On Thursday morning his excursion ticket would force him to go home, and, of course, the Abbey Theatre wouldn't play until Thursday night, which was a pity, for he had vaguely heard of it as queer and interesting, but he couldn't believe that anything could be as good as Mr. Tree or Mr. Robertson.[4]

But the rich theatrical feast he had eagerly looked forward to turned out instead to be somewhat of a disappointment:

. . . secretly; he wouldn't admit it for worlds, for everyone clapped so hard and shouted and there were so many curtain calls—Mr. Tree and *The Red Lamp* were a little disappointing. *Colonel Newcome* was better, for Miss Tree as Kate looked ravishingly beautiful. He slightly regretted at the time (and, of course, bitterly in after years) that they had chosen *The Red Lamp* instead of *Caesar and Cleopatra*—its first performance in Dublin. But anyway, *Mice and Men*, on Wednesday night was just perfect—only, how could anyone break dear "Forby's" heart like that?[5]

Boyishly influenced by Martin Harvey, Robinson then tried to write a novel about a duke and upper-class English society. But his father gently pointed out to him that his knowledge of the aristocracy was limited to watching the local Earl of Bandon getting on or off a Cork train. No wonder Robinson quickly decided to burn his work. Shortly after this setback he attempted a long play for Harvey to act in: "I cannot now remember its subject nor do I know if I ever sent it to him (years after he was to ask me to write a play for him and I was not able to do it, not from any lack of admiration for his work but for lack of subject which would suit him and me), but I know that play I wrote for him must have been on the lines of the *Breed of the Treshams,* or *The Cigarette Maker's Romance* or *The Only Way,* a subject like the English duke, entirely outside my knowledge." [6]

After these fruitless beginnings, an unexpected success came his way when a family friend decided to submit a poem of Robinson from *Contributions* to the *Royal Magazine* in London. Published in the issue for August, 1907, a month before his twenty-first birthday, the magazine gave it a page to itself. From this poem he received his first money as a writer. Encouraged by this response, he wrote many other poems, but by nature he was not a poet, hence all of them were rejected by various magazines.

A day or two after the publication of this poem came the climax of a week which he referred to as "probably the most important week" in his life. Hearing of the visit of the Abbey Theatre Company to Cork, he went to the Saturday afternoon performance at the Opera House.

Robinson had already learned something about the aims and reputation of the company from reading *The Nation.* Even if Synge and Lady Gregory were then only names to him, he, notwithstanding, was quite familiar with Yeats's poetry from the selections in Stopford Brooke's *Anthology of Irish Verse.* Beyond this, in his admiration for Yeats he had selected several of his poems for reprinting in *Contributions;* among these his favorite was "The Hosting of the Sidhe" which had played upon his imagination more than any other poem he had ever read.

Sitting in a warm and almost empty Opera House that memorable August afternoon, he saw the Fays and the Allgoods enact four one-act plays: *Kathleen ni Houlihan, The Hour Glass, The Jackdaw,* and *The Rising of the Moon.* Not recognizing Lady Gregory's one act comedy, *The Jackdaw,* to be a phantasy, he was left bewildered. But Yeats's *Kathleen ni Houlihan* struck home with revolutionary force; it gave Robinson, as he later revealed, a new goal in life and completely and permanently changed his outlook on Ireland: "Certain natural emotions and stirrings, hidden from my family, breathed to the Daunts but discouraged by them were crystallized for ever by *Kathleen ni Houlihan.* . . .

[42]

The Bitterness and Didacticism of the Novice

In my case the conversion was complete, was done in the twenty minutes that Mr. Yeats's play lasted. Those two hours in the pit of the Opera House in Cork made me an Irish dramatist." [7]

The political impressions Robinson received were not the only ones that left an indelible mark upon him. More important to him—since he was never greatly interested in politics as such —was the theatrical world the unique repertoire of the touring Abbey Company unfolded for him. Martin Harvey and the popular sentimental English plays which had previously appealed to him now seemed stale and unreal. For the first time he realized that "here was life, Irish life on the stage, and I had not dreamed that such a thing was possible. . . . It came on me in a flash, as a revelation that play material could be found outside one's own door, at one's fireside. . . . In the future I must 'sing of what I know.' " [8]

The acting of the Company, too, pleasantly surprised him. Up to this he had been accustomed to actors who seemed constantly on the move at the end of their lines. But the Abbey players, as he watched them enact their roles, behaved like human beings: "They moved only when movement was natural and necessary, they used very little gesture and so when a gesture happened it took on great importance. They also spoke beautifully and clearly." [9]

III   The Clancy Name

After these vivid impressions on that August afternoon, Robinson began writing with the Abbey in mind; and, by the end of the year, he had completed a one-act play. About this play he said: "Not for me to copy the poetic prose of *Kathleen ni Houlihan* and *The Hour Glass*, nor the high extravagant comedy of *The Jackdaw*, and when a month or two later I wrote my first Irish play, as instinctively as a wild animal turning to its native food, I wrote a play as harsh as the stones of West Cork, as realistic as the midden in front of an Irish farm house." [10]

The subject of this play, which he called *The Clancy Name*, he found in a short story written by his sister for *Contributions*. Like Colum, Robinson knew of the problems of hard-working, struggling farmers; so he made use of this dramatic substance, giving his play a West-Cork farm setting. He also drew his characters from the country people in that region, a region where the fight of the farmer to eke out a living is more difficult than in Colum's Midlands.

Lady Gregory and Yeats, upon receiving *The Clancy Name*, weighed its merits, and arrived at this decision: "We knew nothing of him, but saw there was good stuff in the play and sent it back with suggestions for strengthening it and getting rid of some unnecessary characters." [11] These improvements Robinson made with alacrity. Then, after what seemed to him to be a portentously long silence, he suddenly received word announcing that *The Clancy Name* would be produced at the Abbey on Thursday, October 8, 1908. The date happened to coincide with his brother's wedding in Dublin, and all the family traveled from Cork for the double event. The Abbey management, however, had forgotten to send complimentary tickets to him for the opening night. Consequently for his first visit to "his spiritual home," he had to sit with his family in the side balcony because he could not afford the higher priced seats downstairs.

The Clancy Name reveals what promises at the outset to be a vital and basic theme for a drama—a struggle between a mother's love and her pride. Mrs. Clancy is determined to uphold the reputable standing of herself and her only offspring, John, among the local farmers. But she has to pay a tragic penalty for her pride in the "Clancy Name," when her son in his moments of mental anguish needs her help.

In the compact story of disillusionment and tragedy that follows, Mrs. Clancy, who has been widowed for some time, assumes the dominant role. By her strenuous efforts and very careful savings, she has been able to reestablish the family name and status in her community, to regain the title to the farm, and to revitalize the land, which her weak but more personable husband had let deteriorate while he was alive. Her constant struggling has made her a determined, shrewd, and intensely proud woman, anxious to have her way at all costs. After keen bargaining over a marriage dowry, she wins a wife for her son John. But fortune favors her only for a short while. John comes home to her in a most harrowed mental state because he has killed a man in a quarrel and hidden the body in a nearby bog. Now he seeks her advice and solace to ease his guilty conscience.

All this disrupts Mrs. Clancy's hopes for continuing the reputation of the family name through her son. Instead of comforting and assisting him in his tormented state, she advises him not to give himself up to the police. Keep the family name without blemish, she entreats, and be quiet about the murder. Here then lies the mother's tragic flaw, her unyielding pride. Both individuals, moreover, are so wrapped up in their separate problems that in their self-pity they ignore their common tragedy:

John   I must do it, it's driving me mad going on this way. Everyone is looking at me and then Jamsey and the blood across his forehead. Didn't I hear you saying a minute ago that you didn't know how anyone could bear it. I must give myself up. I'll swing for it, but I don't care.

Mrs. Clancy   No, you don't care and more shame to you. Look at me that's toiled and worked for five years to pay off the debts on the farm; that's denied myself bite and sup; that's worked morning, noon and night. I've held my head high among the neighbours and now you want to make a disgrace of me. Have you no shame?

John   You said yourself that the man who killed Jamsey should give himself up.

Mrs. Clancy   Ah, but I didn't think then, 'twas a Clancy done it. (coaxingly) I'm not going to let you disgrace me and the Clancy name, John. Think of your father's three brothers, all priests; think of your aunt married to a gentleman in Dublin; think of me a poor widow woman who's always been respected and looked up to by the neighbours. You'll not disgrace me. John, say you won't.

Having well established the conflict in *The Clancy Name,* Robinson fails in the end to bring it to its logical, inevitable outcome —that natural evolution found in the best of tragedies. Rather, he tries an easier solution to his dramatic complication by relying on a melodramatic device to complete his plot.

John goes out, his problem still unresolved, but soon, off-stage there is heard a rapid clattering of horses' feet. A visiting neighbor looks out the window at a runaway horse which has accidentally killed someone. Quickly the suspense is broken. John is brought in dying; he seemingly has given his life to save a young child. John mumbles an attempted confession to ease his guilt, but Mrs. Clancy's pride will not let him be heard. To the assembled neighbors, before the priest comes in, she excuses away her son's last mumblings. Then death comes to him; she has gained her ambition, but at the expense of her son's conscience. By this effective stroke of irony, the author brings the tragedy to a finish. One can see now for the first time a technical gift that he frequently and effectively uses in later plays:

Mrs. Clancy   'Tis no use, he's dead. Look at his teeth clenched on his lips. He'll never speak again, never again, never again, not unless God sent down an angel from Heaven and made him speak. And that'll never be (with a terrible quiet satisfaction). I thank God neither I nor my son have ever brought disgrace on the Clancy name.

Father Murphy   You should be proud this day to be the mother of John Clancy. Let us pray for the soul of John Clancy. . . .

Thus in Robinson's first contribution to the stage one can perceive signs and omens of both his later strengths and weaknesses as a playwright. There is testimony of his adroitness as a structural artist, but there is also evidence of what, in time, acts as a recurring disability: his bent towards melodrama. His technical skill in *The Clancy Name* can be observed in the clever handling of its composition, the tautness acquired from increasing suspense and tragic relief. On the other hand, one obtains a preview of his later tendency to rely either on melodramatic devices, such as the *deus ex machina,* or on his ingenuity as a theatrical craftsman to avoid coming to full grips with whatever dramatic conflict he has to evolve in his more serious plays. As a result he efficiently eases his dramatic burden; but, at the same time, he prevents his dramas from achieving that stamp of inevitability typical of the best and highest tragedies.

His dialogue style, while lacking the poetic luxuriance of Synge, reveals a forceful simplicity and naturalness, winnowed from the uneven flow of daily casual talk. He also allows some unforced humor to rise to the surface as a source of relief during the play's somber moments. In doing so, he foreshadows his later ability as a writer of comedy in Irish life. One of these light scenes, for instance, involves two of the Clancy neighbors who are discussing the murder before Mrs. Clancy arrives on the scene:

Mrs. Spillane   As I was saying, the police needn't go a mile beyond Brien's farm to find out the truth about Jamsey.

The Bitterness and Didacticism of the Novice

Eugene   Well, well. Still Benjamin's a quiet man, except when he has the drink taken.

Mrs. Spillane   I never said it was Benjamin done it, and don't you be going and putting it on me saying that I did. You're a queer man, Eugene, the notions you do pick up.

Eugene   (apologetically) You said no such thing indeed; it is only what I was thinking myself.

Though Robinson's plays, unlike those of his famous predecessor Synge, did not lead to any political or literary repercussions, his one-act drama, for a beginner's work, stirred the critics to considerable controversy. The adverse criticism seemed quite surprising since the audience liked *The Clancy Name* on the opening night. Yet the next day, *The Freeman's Journal* fell upon it, violently asserting that the play besmirched a very respectable family name in Ireland.[12] Henderson, then secretary to the Abbey, amusingly explained in his diary that the severe review was caused by the supperless and hungry critic's having to wait too long to see the new production, the third on the program.[13] The attack in *The Freeman's Journal* led to more critical sparks. Stephen Gwynn, one of the early supporters of the Irish Literary Theatre, who was then unknown to Robinson, rallied to the play's defense; and *The Leader* joined in the melee, belligerently proclaiming, "The man who wrote about [the play] in the 'Freeman' is an ass." [14]

Conscious of the criticism directed toward the harshness of *The Clancy Name*, and after suggestions for altering it came from Yeats, Robinson decided to soften its tone. The resulting new version was played at the Abbey, September 30, 1909, and two years later it was published along with *Harvest*. Of the play in its initial form no copy exists, but from the memoirs and clippings of the Dublin diarist and historian of the Irish theatrical scene, Joseph Holloway, one can gather some idea of the original work. The ending of the first edition was more prolonged, allowing Mrs. Clancy to show more contending emotions than in the revisal. George Fitzmaurice, an Abbey playwright in the Synge tradition, who saw both versions enacted, considered the first one better; the second seemed too machinemade and smooth.

The Clancy Name was brought to the attention of Mrs. Brown-Potter, who had come to Dublin to play in *Lady Frederick* at the Gaiety Theatre. Impressed during the improved performance of the second night, she asked Robinson's permission to produce the play in French in a leading Paris theatre. But he did not feel attracted to the offer, for "flattering as that might be, I knew instinctively that plays for Mrs. Brown-Potter and her sort were not for the likes of me to write." [15]

IV The Cross Roads

After the production of *The Clancy Name*, Robinson decided to stay for a few weeks at Bray, a small resort near Dublin, spending his time either going to the Abbey or sitting on the Bray esplanade writing the second and least successful of all his dramas, *The Cross Roads*. Originally named *Cross Ways* it had two acts and a prologue. These he wrote backwards, the last act first, and the prologue last; his work he later described as "peasant tragedy of the most realistic, ruthless kind." [16]

Shortly after his return to West Cork in October, he submitted his new play for the judgment of the Abbey Board of Directors. Three months later, when Yeats wrote giving tentative approval of the play, Robinson became apprehensive lest the Dublin newspaper critics again confuse fact with fiction in their reviews. To protect himself, he checked the setting of his play by writing to Henderson at the Abbey on February 25, 1909, two days before his play was put into rehearsal: "I am very glad the prologue pleased Mr. Yeats. ₀ . . Don't you think it would be well to look in a Dublin directory and see if there is any such club in Dublin as the Erin Club. We don't want a libel action." [17]

After a week's postponement because of Synge's death, *The Cross Roads* was acted for the first time on April 1, 1909, at the Abbey. With this drama Robinson enters on a campaign of reform, in which he endeavors to justify his critical opinions of some of the facets of Irish life he disliked, and in this way help the recovery of his native land. He now gives full attention to a situation partially touched upon in *The Clancy Name*: the loveless marriages contracted among farmers' families in Ireland either for financial gain or security. To enlarge the background for this subject, he introduces a subsidiary problem: the attempt of the government to spread new agricultural ideas among the farmers to improve their lot.

The playwright tries to prove his Ibsenesque main thesis by unfolding a study of the loveless union of a progressive, intelligent farm girl, Ellen McCarthy, with a boorish farmer.

The prologue, set in the Dublin clubhouse of the Erin Debating Society, an organization for young people interested in politics and economics, shows that Ellen, more or less in the manner of Ibsen's emancipated women, has socially and intellectually advanced herself in the city after putting her experiences there to good use. At the same time, she still retains an interest in bettering the condition of her farm home in West Cork. While she is active in the Club, she meets an idealistic and ambitious young writer, Brian O'Connor. He falls in love with her, but she does not fully return his affections. Into the web of the story the playwright at this point unexpectedly inserts a curse that can befall any person who enters into wedlock for worldly advantage and thereby frustrates "true-love" marriages. Then, after the curse is stated, the speaker is heard of no more in the play.

Ellen is not much impressed by these dire omens, and she feels that her mother's farm in Cork would offer her an ideal place to serve her country in a more practical way through the introduction of efficient, modern farming methods in her own community. Her actions, she believes, will do far more to ameliorate the lives of her neighbors than all the talk she had listened to in Dublin.

In the first act, all goes well for the industrious Ellen in her new life on the farm in Ballygurteen, County Cork. Her plans have become so successful that the neighbors begin to follow her wise example. Brian, who has now advanced himself in Dublin, pays her a visit to urge her to become his wife; but she will not accept his offer. She intends to continue her service to her country by accepting the match her mother has arranged with Tom Dempsey, son of a comparatively flourishing farmer. She suggests that Brian come back in seven years.

In the last act, seven years later, a complete reversal of fortune has afflicted Ellen. She looks aged and shabby; and, although her neighbors are thriving, a long litany of disasters has stricken her household. Her husband has taken to drink and sourly blames her for bringing a black curse on him ever since he married her.

Brian, meanwhile, remembering Ellen's suggestion, again visits her, only to find her in this wretched state; he becomes disgusted with her husband and suggests that she return with him to Dublin. Again at the crossroads, she decides—unlike Ibsen's heroine, Nora, in *The Doll's House*—to cling to her unhappy lot, even though numerous adversities loom ahead. The anticipated misfortunes may perhaps be just as satisfactory as living on the edge of a precipice, as many of Ibsen's emancipated women seem to do when they sadly leave their one-set-play-sphere to enter loveless and lonely into their new world.

Once again Robinson concludes with an effective, but melodramatically painful scene, as Brian departs, and the husband decides to get drunk at a local public house:

Ellen   What are you doing? (Frightened)

Tom   I'll tell you what I'm doing. I'm locking the door the way you won't go out after that young man; an I'm going to step down to the village now for a sup of drink. An then I'm coming back; and by God I'll make you pay for the night's work, Ellen McCarthy, till you'd wish you were dead for the black curse you brought on this farm . . . . an for the liking you have to the young man. (goes out). [Ellen remains sitting at the table, staring in front of her with sad, hopeless eyes. The key turns in the lock with a sound of dreadful finality.]

In retrospect, then, one can see that the impression created by the author lacks a unifying principle and that the problem he poses lies unsolved. He has failed to persuade his audience that his climax is the natural result of a loveless marriage. In fact, one's ordinary experience and one's sense of justice protest that the outcome of the play should be different. His denouément depends on a most improbable and arbitrary assumption. Ellen's advanced economic ideas fail, but her neighbors prosper. His handling of expository dialogue, moreover, indicates that he has not yet fully mastered Ibsen's retrospective technique. And the curse, fleetingly mentioned in the prologue but leading to all the disaster, is an obvious *deus ex machina*. Yet in the play's favor one can perceive that the action is supported by natural, well-sustained dialogue—an aptitude of Robinson that improved with time.

The Cross Roads, despite these weaknesses, gained the approval of Abbey audiences; truly, it had, as Robinson conceded, a success beyond its deserts largely owing to the magnificent acting of Sara Allgood, Arthur Sinclair, and Maire O'Neill.[18] It also won recognition, Robinson believed, ". . . because it and its small elder brother brought for the first time on the Irish stage harsh reality. It was part and parcel of what the young generation was beginning to think about Ireland. For a hundred years we had been engaged in political struggle after political struggle. . . . We wrote sentimental poems about ourselves, and then came the Parnell debacle. From the foundations the country now had to build anew. . . . We must criticise ourselves ruthlessly." [19]

In this estimate of the value and purpose of his play, one can note a wide difference between Robinson's interpretation of its significance and that of Yeats when he decided to accept it for the Abbey. The latter's opinions show him divided between his original idea of what Irish drama should be like and the need to encourage the new realism:

We accepted the play because of its central idea; a seeming superstition of its creator, a promise of a new attitude towards life, of something beyond logic. . . . They misunderstood Robinson's idea, luckily for its popularity; and so turned all into the commonplace. They allow their minds to dwell so completely on the logic that they do not notice what as it were swims upon it or juts up from its river bed. . . . Robinson should become a celebrated dramatist if the theatre lasts long enough. He does not argue like the imitators of Ibsen, though his expression of life is as logical, hence his grasp on active passion. Passion is logic when bent on action.[20]

Robinson, at all events, since he was conscious of the play's defects, decided to create a new version. While in the process of reshaping his play, an unexpected newspaper controversy arose concerning the influence Yeats had over Abbey playwrights in seeking for revisions of their works. This was the only argument of its kind Robinson ever entered into, for, after it was over, he followed Yeats's advice about the fruitlessness of engaging in newspaper debates. J. J. O'Neill, a bibliographer and historian of the Irish theatre, challenged Robinson to defend himself regarding Yeats's power over him. In the discussion that ensued in *The Cork Sportsman*, Robinson, from his Cork home, wrote on December 15, 1909: "Since April 1st, I have made many alterations in the play; it has now reached a form which fairly satisfies me. . . . I cannot let the impression get abroad that I have any reason to be dissatisfied with the directors' treatment of me. Both my plays owe much to their advice and help."

O'Neill, finding that Robinson's letter failed to clarify satisfactorily the point in dispute, replied from Dublin on December 20, 1909:

Shall I tell you the secret of the unnecessary revision. It reveals the controlling hand of Mr. Yeats. Hardly one of its [the Abbey's] plays, but has been seriously altered since its first production. . . . To throw dust into the public eye, so that it may dwell on this personal idiosyncrasy, he brings his strong will to bear upon those dramatists who have rallied to his movement to induce them to fall in line and tinker at their accepted plays. If they fail to yield to pressure, their pieces are shelved. That probably is the secret of Mr. Robinson's revised version of a play that needed no revising and will probably be spoiled by over touching.

Later, O'Neill's judgment on *The Cross Roads* apparently was substantiated in a way by Robinson, for he did not issue an edition of the new condensed version but published his original work. The play in its new form, produced on February 3, 1910, at the Abbey, was reduced to two acts by the elimination of the awkward prologue. The alterations, nevertheless, do not improve any of the major deficiencies already noted in the earlier script. The condensation in size forces the author to account more fully for Ellen's fate within the limits of the two acts; but the curse, still included, is uttered this time by Brian. He cautions Ellen that the frustration of nature will lead to harmful consequences. On his next visit to see her, he reminds her of his warning.

The somber atmosphere of harsh realism tinged with irony that persists throughout the dramas of the playwright's earlier days was briefly relieved by a one-act farce called *The Lesson of His Life*. This playlet about country life was enacted by the Cork Dramatic Society which was then trying to do for that city what the Abbey was doing for Dublin. Being an amusing piece, it was well received at its opening at the Dun Theatre, Cork, on December 2, 1909. Since this work was not published, the extant script has the chief value now of giving a sample of Robinson's earliest work as a writer of comedy. The same program also included the apprentice efforts of two other "Cork Realists" who

later wrote for the Abbey, T. C. Murray and the versatile Daniel
Corkery. In connection with this performance and Robinson's
association with the Cork Little Theatre movement, Corkery recalled that Robinson "contrasted with us all personally—we were
all Catholics connected with the Gaelic League. His education
had been otherwise. Still we all liked him, although differing in
politics and almost every other deep old attitude." [21]

V *First Appointment to the Abbey*

During late fall or early winter of 1909 occurred another outstanding event in Robinson's life. He received an invitation from
Lady Gregory and Yeats to visit them in Dublin to discuss some
new projects they had in mind for the Abbey. For Robinson's first
meeting with the famous pair, Yeats came late, being held
up at a rehearsal. Meanwhile Lady Gregory, dressed very plainly
in black and wearing her pince-nez, tried to put him at ease
during the interview. She chatted first about Yeats's exceptional
revisions on *The Golden Helmet,* and then went on to ask Robinson about his family, his background, and his education. The wide
difference in their ages, she was almost fifty-eight and he was
twenty-three, made him think of her as an old woman.

Yeats upon his arrival immediately broke into a prepared and
possibly rehearsed speech for Robinson's benefit. He elaborated
about the Norwegian Theatre at Bergen that, on realizing Ibsen's
genius, had taken him from a job in a chemist's shop and had
given him a responsible position at the age of twenty-three. Robinson, too, was the same age and was similarly inexperienced. A
dramatist, Yeats continued, should know his instrument, and
work in the theatre would shape him as a better dramatist. Yeats
brought the discussion to a head by asking if Robinson had any
plans for his future. He had none, so Yeats offered him the post of
producer of plays and manager at a salary of £150 a year. The
young man was naturally delighted at the prospect. It was, he
said, "fantastical, I knew next to nothing of the theatre, I had a
very poor education, I couldn't add up figures. But if Mr. Yeats
was crazy, I was not and I accepted on the spot." [22]

Robinson's appointment to the Abbey led to an amusing tale in
Dublin about how Yeats decided to select him, even though he
scarcely knew him. One evening at the Abbey, Yeats, sitting
directly behind Robinson, was fascinated by the shape of the

back of his head. Turning to Lady Gregory, he exclaimed, "This man's head is very interesting from the rear. He looks just like the man we're looking for. We must make him our next manager." Yeats held that this story was true, but Robinson always doubted it.

Closer to the truth was the fact that the Abbey needed a new manager and producer to replace Norreys Connell; he had resigned in July, 1909, under pressure from Miss Horniman, the generous English benefactress of the Abbey, whose help had provided that theatre with the necessary funds to open its doors. Both Yeats and Lady Gregory, moreover, were conscious not only that Robinson showed increasing promise as a playwright but that he was young enough to mold and thus fit in with their policies and hopes for the future of the Abbey.

Yeats had every reason to be pleased with the soundness of his judgment. Robinson was tireless in his efforts to promote the interests of the Abbey. Also, his gentle but firm manner served him well as its producer and manager. Soon he emerged in the significant role of "general trouble shooter" for the Abbey, patching up rivalries among the actors, placating sensitive and angry authors, or nagging the easygoing ones to complete their plays. Unquestionably he behaved—as his colleague the Ulster dramatist, Rutherford Mayne once remarked—"like a sort of hospitable Abbot of his Abbey showing American and English visitors around." [23]

Robinson's parents, happy at their son's good fortune, wrote to him in Dublin evaluating his new job. His father, as might be expected, advised him that "the theatrical profession no doubt has drawbacks and temptations of various kinds, but I trust by God's grace you will be kept in the way of religion and goodness." His practical mother added her reservations and suggestions: "I think they are getting you cheap. I also somewhat dread that your own literary work may be hindered by routine work. You ought to order at least four evening shirts. . . . I think you will want warmer vests. London is very cold and so is Dublin." [24]

To offset the inexperience of the new manager, Yeats had planned for him quite an intensive program for observing and studying the methods of some of the best English directors in the London theatre at that time. The moment was ripe for experiencing such training, since the intellectual theatre was then very active. Charles Frohman had begun his repertory company at the Duke of York Theatre, with Granville-Barker, Dion Boucicault, and Bernard Shaw as his stage directors. Among the new productions expected early in 1910 were plays by Galsworthy and Granville-Barker, a couple by Barrie, and Shaw's *Misalliance.*

Because Shaw had always been a friend to the Abbey, Yeats wrote to him asking his cooperation in the new plans for the Irish theatre. Shaw wired back favorably, saying he would make Robinson his nominal secretary. A few days later Robinson was on his way to London. On Robinson's arrival, Shaw acted as his intermediary with Granville-Barker, who readily agreed to allow Robinson to watch his rehearsals. Writing from Adelphi Terrace on February 3, 1910, Shaw informed Robinson of the arrangements: "Granville-Barker says you may come to any of his rehearsals you please. He rehearses tomorrow at 10 at the Globe. If you go there and ask for him (send up your card), he will have you passed in, but if you would like to call here at 9:30 I daresay I could catch him before he goes out and introduce you to him. . . ." [25]

And so the way was paved for what to Robinson were magical weeks in London. He stayed with Yeats in his flat at Woburn Buildings, with its rooms decorated in blues and browns and lit by candles, its walls lined with shelves of enticing books and hung with Blake's engravings. Robinson achieved the main purpose of his visit while attending both morning and afternoon rehearsals at the Duke of York or dress rehearsals late at night. He was able to watch and to compare the methods of three important producers and to evaluate their merits and defects. The time was well spent; to his innate sense of the theatre he added the valuable experience of practical stage training from outstanding instructors. No longer would he be ignorant of what he should do in his new position.

Though a great admirer of Shaw's works and much impressed by Shaw's personality, Robinson did not quite approve of Shaw's cult of efficiency or of the fact that Shaw thought more of his play than of his actors. Years afterwards, talking to Archibald Henderson, Shaw's biographer, Robinson told him that Shaw while producing *Misalliance* taught him only one thing, "the actor must speak his lines with enunciation so accurate as to be heard easily in the remotest corner of the play house." [26]

Robinson regarded Boucicault as the most sensible and practical but the least imaginative of the three. Granville-Barker thoroughly impressed him, notably his rehearsal device of a stage-cloth marked off like a huge chess board. On this the speeches, gestures, and moves of the actors were carefully planned. It was the work of a genius, said Robinson, "but each player was expected to imitate the intonation of the producer's, and in the end *The Madras House* came on the stage a beautiful but dead thing." [27]

Whatever free time Robinson had was spent omnivorously reading the many works of contemporary writers in Yeats's library. Lady Gregory, on a visit to London at the time, took further interest in him, acting as his social guide; her society friends introduced an element of sophistication to the social life of this inexperienced young man from the Irish provinces. She also expanded his knowledge of the theatre by taking him to many of the plays then running in London, such as *Beethoven* with Beerbohm Tree and *The Blue Bird*. Best of all he admired the passionate peasant dramas of Grasso and his Sicilian players. She even encouraged him, but without success, to take up boxing lessons so that he could handle drunks and disorderlies at the Abbey.

Before Robinson left London, Granville-Barker called him aside and counseled him to make sure that the producer's name always appeared on the program. Since then the Abbey has followed Barker's advice.

Having gained confidence from his London schooling, Robinson was back in Dublin by March, 1910, to take up his first assignment at the Abbey. At Yeats's request, he began directing a revival of Boyle's *The Eloquent Dempsey*. It was obvious that Robinson showed dislike for this comedy of small town life. And Yeats grew a little nervous about the debut of his protégé. Would Robinson effectively cope, Yeats wondered, with such accomplished and gifted actors as Sara Allgood, Maire O'Neill, Arthur Sinclair, Fred Donovan, and J. M. Kerrigan. But Yeats brightened considerably when Robinson told him of Granville-Barker's chess board stage cloth. "Get one painted at once," Yeats urged.

"That will terrify them. You will have complete authority over
them."

The next play on Robinson's schedule was a first production of
Padraic Colum's *Thomas Muskerry* for May 5 of the same year.
He arrived about an hour late at the theatre for the first-reading
rehearsal with the Company, after being delayed at his apartment in some preliminary talk with Colum about changes in the
play's construction. Yeats, already waiting in the Abbey stalls to
direct the launching of Colum's drama, was irked and severely
criticized Robinson for his tardy arrival. It was a reprimand
Robinson never forgot, for he was afterwards noted for his almost
"inhuman punctuality" in his rehearsal appointments. Even dress
rehearsals, for instance, he would not allow to be any more than
half an hour late in starting.

A month or two later, George Moore asked Robinson, who
lived near him in Dublin at the time, if he would cooperate with
him in adapting *Esther Waters* for the stage. Moore had been toy-
ing with the idea for some time but had given up the task. He
told Robinson that he had seen his *The Cross Roads* and that its
realism had not only appealed to him but also revived his hopes
for dramatizing his novel. Flattered at Moore's request, Robinson
readily consented to assist as best as he could, and found the
novelist's cosmopolitan habits and tastes delightful. Moore, then
working on his *Hail and Farewell*, typically tried to impress
Robinson with his real or imaginary love intrigues. One evening,
in particular, when Robinson was admiring Moore's luxurious
fur lined and collared coat, the novelist said to him rather
gravely, "That, Robinson, is the reward of ten years adultery." [28]

Moore visited Robinson in his apartment nearly every afternoon to inspect the progress made on the script. The novelist's
interest grew, and he accelerated his writing tempo until the
five acts were finished. Robinson contributed the second act,
set in the kitchen of a cottage where illegitimate children are
farmed out. It was written, he said, in his most realistic West-
Cork manner. Comparing this act with its source, one can note
that Robinson has quite successfully dramatized it. Yet, when the
play was acted the following year in London, Moore forgot
about his agreement to acknowledge Robinson's assistance and
gave him no recognition on the program.

Robinson held no grudge against Moore; and, when he next

met him in London, he invited him to join Yeats and himself for supper after the theatre. Yeats and Moore were then not on the best of terms, so Robinson was quite amused at the battle of personalities that ensued. While Moore groped for the right word to devastate his opponent, Yeats, whose mind worked quickly in verbal exchange, darted ahead to some other topic leaving Moore fumbling behind.

VI Harvest

Robinson returned to his role of crusading reformer in *Harvest*, the first of his own plays that he directed. He penned it during the autumn and winter of 1909 while living at home in Cork. Appropriately enough its opening night at the Abbey on May 19, 1910, was wet and gloomy. A goodly crowd attended this performance, enthusiastically applauding the merits of the actors; and the author "when called, walked hurriedly across the stage as if he feared that hisses were in store for him as well as approval. One noted a frightened air about the way he took his call." [29] There were, however, some trenchant dissenting opinions in the audience: George Moore could see nothing to admire in it, Padraic Colum thought it much worse than his *Thomas Muskerry*, and the editor of the *Evening Telegraph* argued that Robinson should have his neck wrung for writing such a play.

The object of Robinson's propaganda in this play is the converse of that which Tolstoi formulated in *The Power of Darkness:* that the lack of education among illiterate peasants brings a moral decadence in its wake. Robinson, in contrast, believes that it is very unwise to give an academic curriculum to people living on the land because it leads to their moral downfall; it is better and more natural for them to cling to farm life. Taken out of their native sphere by the wrong schooling, the sons and daughters of Irish farmers only become unhappy, dissolute, and physically decadent. The author seeks to demonstrate this point in his picture of the lives of an aged Cork farmer, Tim Hurley, and his children.

Old Tim Hurley has slaved all his life to give his offspring what he considers the best education for their future, and his neighbors respect him as a model farmer for his sacrifice. But, unknown to them, his efforts to benefit his children have impoverished his farm. The local teacher, Mr. Lordan, has esteemed the young Hurleys as his prize pupils, and he hopes to advance them on the road to future social success. Of all the family, only one son, Maurice, stays behind to assist his father on the farm. Since old Tim needs some outside aid to keep the farm going, he assumes that his fortunate progeny will rally to his assistance.

But their response is almost negligible: Tim, a priest in America, is too busy collecting funds for the Church; Pat, a secretary to an English nobleman, has become a snob, leading him to change his name and religion; Bob, a lawyer, has social aspirations that keep him continually in debt; Mary, her employer's mistress in England, enjoys greater comforts than she had while his typist; Jack, an assistant to a chemist in Dublin, has married out of his class. All have their excuses.

The father, when he receives such discouraging responses from his educated children, becomes so anxious to save his farm from bankruptcy that he decides to burn a barn to collect the insurance money on it. Jack makes a partial gesture when he offers the help of his wife and himself in running the farm, for they are both romantic about the rewards of farming. But in a short while he realizes that he is now completely unfit for the farming life and throws it up in disgust:

Jack   I hope I'll never see this cursed place again: before a month there'll be a few thousand miles of clean salt water between me and Ireland. Ireland! I hate the very word.

Mary, who has come home to recapture the unique satisfaction she had of old on the farm, also finds life there is not as she had imagined while in exile. Her father's criminal act snuffs out her dream. She makes up her mind to return to her London lover, her once consoling fancies now merely ironic delusions. To her brother Jack she confides how strong is the allure of her past life:

Mary   I'm not happy here. I thought if I could get home to the farm and the old simple life it would be all right but it isn't. I always thought if I could get away to Knockmalglass, I could start fair again. But Jack, the dreadful thing is I want to go back. I can't give it up. I'm longing for that life, and its excitement and splendour and colour. . . . Oh Jack, I want it all, all that dreadfully splendid life (with a last brilliant smile she goes out).

Before she returns to England, she lessens the financial worries of her father by getting money from her lover. But she pretends to Maurice and her father that Pat sent it. This gift and the dishonest insurance money bring about brighter prospects for the family at home.

Again one finds a bitterly ironic conclusion which involves the unfortunate, utterly naïve schoolmaster, who symbolizes the evil spirit of education. Earlier in the play, Maurice had insulted him because of the results of his teaching: "I'd take you up on the quarry and break your bloody neck." Now at the play's end, Maurice, thinking that Mary's contribution had come from one of his brothers, turns to the teacher to apologize:

Maurice   Here's my hand Mr. Lordan. . . . It's only today I'm beginning to understand what a terrible lot we owe to you.

Lordan   Not at all, Maurice, not at all. I only did the little I could—it wasn't much—I wish it was more.

It is difficult, just the same, to believe that the education the family received has caused all this spiritual and physical vitiation. The thesis, too, is very much in disagreement with actual conditions in Ireland. The playwright, the artist as lay preacher, cannot afford to give a balanced image; he must always favorably color his point of view. Robinson's characters thus become merely puppets forced into unnatural situations and very much at the mercy of his didacticism. Ironically enough, the best-drawn character in the play is Maurice, the boy who stays at home on the farm.

The third act shows the effect of this strain in its marked deterioration in quality. An air of unreality hangs over it. The scene, already mentioned, in which Mary tells about her sordid life in London, suggests that the author is floundering in unknown waters. She acts quite like one of the new young women of the drama of that time confessing to the error of her ways.

When evaluating his play many years afterwards, Robinson, severely criticized the defects in its structure: "*Harvest,* my third play, was not a good one. . . . It had some shocking faults of construction; the play began with a scene between two brothers who sit on a wall and tell each other facts about themselves and their family, facts perfectly well known to each of them. It was a beautifully easy way of putting the audience *au fait* with the situation, but quite absurd. I remember Moore gently chiding my naiveté. . . . Sometimes I wish we could go back to olden times when the programme told the audience so much." [30] Besides these flaws in the play's form, one cannot but feel dissatisfied with the atmosphere of gloom and acrimony hovering over it. Another point, all the serious creations of his noviceship are similarly burdened. One finds that the country people in his dramas—as he himself confirmed—are for the most part avaricious, mean, drunk, and brutal. The spirit of his writing up to now suggests at times the disposition of a frustrated young crusader who sees little hope for his ideals being fulfilled in an unheeding world. His work also lies—as does that of Synge before him—under the shadow of the glum and pessimistic Naturalism of the Continental and English theatre at the turn of the twentieth century.

Despite their inadequacies, his first plays were so admired by other young writers that they evoked, Robinson contended, a series of grimly critical plays: "We were very young and we shrunk from nothing. We knew our Ibsen and the plays of the Lancashire school, we showed our people as robbers and murderers, guilty of arson, steeped in trickery and jobbery." [31]

In confirmation of this statement, A. P. Wilson revealed later, when lecturing on his duties as general manager at the Abbey, that, on a rough average, nineteen out of every twenty plays submitted to the Abbey Theatre were more or less realistic in nature; dealt with peasant life; and, out of the nineteen, almost all were usually morbid.

Under this influence, for example, came T. C. Murray, one of Robinson's notable contemporaries. He attributed his first realization of the tragic in people's lives to seeing *The Cross Roads,* which led him to write his first Abbey play, *Birthright,* produced in 1910.

Not all the Irish literary world approved of this trend in Irish drama. Its morbidly realistic qualities did not appeal, in particular, to one of the most prominent figures in the Irish Literary Renaissance, George Russell, who was moved to protest: "All this is helping in our national pessimism and self mistrust." [32]

CHAPTER 3

The Romantic in Politics

YEATS'S criticism of Robinson for being late at the first rehearsal of Colum's *Thomas Muskerry* was nothing compared with the repercussions that arose for the Abbey and Robinson on May 7, 1910, the third day of its performance. The British King, Edward VII, had died unexpectedly on the previous night, and his death put the young and inexperienced but nationalistic minded Robinson in a quandary. He was puzzled about what bearing the death of Edward could have on the Irish national theatre. He could not consult with Yeats, who was visiting Maude Gonne in Normandy, or with Lady Gregory, who was at her Galway home. So, with the support of the players, he decided to keep the Abbey open, even though all the other Dublin theatres were closed because of the King's death. In a subsequent letter to Yeats he explained what occurred:

You have asked me to tell you what happened on May 7th last. I read in the morning papers of the King's death, but I never thought of the effect it would have on the theatres and places of amusement. However, about 11.15 [sic] our secretary came to my rooms and told me that he heard that the other theatres in Dublin were closing and asked me what we should do. I knew that the Abbey Theatre had been carried on from the beginning as a purely artistic venture, I knew that its policy was to ignore politics, and I thought that if we closed we would be throwing ourselves definitely on one political side and that we should remain open taking no notice of a circumstance that had no significance to the arts. However, I decided to leave the matter to Lady Gregory and wired to her as follows: "Theatres closing here. What am I to do? I think we should remain open but leave decision to you."

This was handed in ten minutes before twelve. I then went to the Theatre and waited for a reply; none came, and I decided to go on with the matinée. Lady Gregory's answer desiring the Theatre to be closed came in the course of the afternoon—in the interval before the last act of the play we were performing. "Should close through courtesy. A. Gregory."

It was too late to stop the matinée then, and the good audience encouraged me to think that little criticism would be passed on our having remained open. It was too late to put notices in the evening papers cancelling the night performances and if there was any crime in having played we had already committed it.[1]

Considerable trouble immediately developed for Robinson and for the Abbey when Miss Horniman learned of his action. Although sympathetic to Yeats's aspirations for the growth of a uniquely Irish theatre, she was opposed to the spirit of Irish nationalism. Such being the case, she regarded Robinson's decision as a deliberate political insult to England. She then irately demanded his dismissal from his post at the Abbey, else she would deprive it of her financial support. Even though the subsidy would have ended anyway in nine months, the directors of the theatre closed the theatre on the day of the King's funeral but refused to accede to her request to drop Robinson. Whereupon she withdrew her grant of £600. They then sued for the money; and, when the case was submitted to the *Manchester Guardian* for arbitration, its editor, C. P. Scott, awarded the decision to the Abbey directors—much to the delight of Arthur Griffith and the nationalist press. But Yeats and Lady Gregory thought it a more fitting gesture to free Miss Horniman from her debt; so, in the main, the affair ended fairly reasonably for all concerned.

Because the episode weighed on Robinson's mind, he sought to make amends through assuming the added job of secretary and extra responsibilities at the theatre without any increase in pay. From then on, the activities of the Abbey and his own became so entwined that his autobiography, *Curtain Up*, written in 1942, almost reads like a history of the Abbey. This devotion to duty was not in vain. It helped him to widen further his growing practical understanding of the many facets of the theatre and to acquire, at the same time, valuable attainments in his career as a playwright: "Now I was at the theatre at half past nine in the morning answering letters and lodging the previous night's receipts, then rehearsals and rehearsals, then front-of-the-house man at night counting the house and checking the money. Certainly, I was learning to know my theatre." [2]

I *On Tour with the Abbey Theatre*

Though the Abbey had a very reputable group of players and an excellent repertory of plays when Robinson began his regime as manager-producer, it had not yet gained the popularity which it was to acquire later. Attendance was sparse, the stalls were generally almost empty, only the cheaper seats were frequented. For this disappointing condition Robinson blamed certain snobbish social traits of Dublin audiences: "Dublin is one of the most snobbish cities in the world and the fact that the Abbey plays were written by almost unknown Irishmen and Irishwomen made them not worth serious consideration. . . . The players at the Abbey were all Irish, worse still were mainly from Dublin." [3]

This lack of public support worsened the financial encumbrances of the Abbey, and the Company was compelled to seek revenue from annual tours to the larger English cities and to the university towns of Oxford and Cambridge, where they were given almost limitless hospitality. Robinson joined the players on these journeys, and, abetted by the favorable reviews of the perceptive London and Manchester critics, they received rather complimentary response from English audiences. In London, for their six-week season of Irish plays, the Abbey Company attracted to its productions many of the most intellectual and fashionable people in the capital, vying in popularity with such visiting companies as the Russian opera and ballet. When its members were also asked to play at Buckingham Palace, they thought it wise to refuse; but, at the invitation of one of the housemasters, they enacted *Kathleen ni Houlihan* in the cloisters of Eton College.

The visits to London afforded Robinson many opportunities for exploring the current theatrical fare there. Once, as the guest of Shaw in his box for a performance of the ballet, Robinson was much surprised to note that Shaw was horrified at the scantiness of the men's costumes.

These English journeys put the theatre back on its feet financially; it even managed to save some money. Encouraged by these results, the directors, who had long desired such a visit, planned to take the plays to America. Shortly afterwards, in September, 1911, Yeats, Robinson, and the company left for their first trip to America with the most pleasant prospects before them, only to find their expectations rudely upset. Actually, the Irish-American friends they had anticipated meeting there greeted them with brickbats. But one must try, said Robinson, to understand the psychology of the Irish-American point of view: "Irish-America had made a pipe dream of Ireland. . . . There should have been old fashioned roses round the door and inside there should be a turf-fire and an old granny in white cap gently stirring it and crooning softly. Instead, we gave them a harsh, realistic setting, small farmhouses, a smell of dung coming through the door, and after as in *The Cross Roads* a fire black-out." [4]

Boston, New York, Philadelphia, and Chicago, where the Irish in large numbers had made their homes, saw reenacted the same tumultuous happenings once aroused by *The Playboy* in Dublin. This battle against the Company lasted all through its tour. But Lady Gregory and Robinson made effective partners, winning every fight for the freedom of the theatre.

The Abbey Company opened at the new Plymouth Theatre in Boston in September, but before long the Gaelic societies there were damning as anti-Christian writers both Robinson and Lady Gregory, who had just arrived to join the company. Shaw came to their defense when the Central Council of the Irish County Associations of Greater Boston asserted that the Council members knew their Ireland as children did their mother. In an interview in the *New York Sun,* Shaw retorted that this was "not a very happy bit of rhetoric because children never do know their mothers." Encouraging Robinson and the players also was Vachel Lindsay; he unexpectedly visited Robinson at his hotel room and chanted his poetry while perched on the side of Robinson's bed.

After Boston the Company moved to the Maxine Elliot Theatre in New York, where Robinson assisted the police in ejecting excited disturbers from the lobby. For once, though, at the Christmas Day performance in New York, *The Playboy* was enacted without any trouble. Just the same, Maire Nic Shiubhlaigh, one of the fifteen members of the Company, recalled in her book, *The Splendid Years,* that the players were a forlorn, homesick little group that night, with no letters, no Christmas cards, no gifts from Ireland. But "Robinson, tall and a little shy, came down from the theatre office, his arms laden with parcels; handed us all something from himself: books, cosmetics, handkerchiefs for the girls; pipes, walking sticks, ties for the men. It was one of those things we remembered." [5]

Next, in Philadelphia, the Company was brought to court for presenting indecent plays but was exonerated through the skillful legal aid of Yeats's friend, John Quinn. Finally, in Chicago, Robinson and Lady Gregory were personally threatened, the latter receiving a menacingly melodramatic note: "Your doom is sealed."

In this manner, the Irish in America protested against the shattering of their dream world through the realism of the plays presented by the visitors from the homeland. Despite the intensity of these attacks—these "lovers' quarrels" as Robinson styled them—the players and the plays brought further renown to the Abbey and to Ireland. And instead of staying for three months, as originally planned, the Company contracted to prolong its visit to six months. In fact, so heartening were the financial results that the Company chose to return to the United States in the autumn of 1912, within six months of their return from the first voyage.

II Patriots

During this period of Robinson's writing career, chiefly after his return from his visits to England and the United States, one can observe the beginnings of a change in his attitude towards his dramatic material. Less and less does he critically interpret Irish life in terms of sharp irony and stark realism; more and more does he find solace in the blossoming hopes for Irish political freedom. And these consolations lead him to soften his youthful discontent with conditions in Ireland. To a considerable extent this change can also be traced to the potent molding influence of Yeats, whom Robinson admiringly called "the dominant personality in my life."

In his earlier days, Yeats, as befitting a poet, was enamored of an Ireland of dreams; and he colored his orthodox nationalism with a romantic hue. This romanticism was not restricted to the poet alone; it always lay inherent in the nationalistic aspirations of the Irish people, not only acting as an encouragement against despair but as a consolation against dire poverty. Yeats, who had been first awakened into political action by the idealistic appeal of O'Leary's nationalism, wished to unite the two separate entities in Ireland, Gaelic-Ireland and Anglo-Ireland, into a common political cause, so that neither might "shed its pride." Since Yeats tended to see history in terms of its leaders, he sought some Irish models to inspire him in his political aims. So he selected from the Protestant line of Irish patriots two particularly dramatic figures for his admiration: Parnell, for his aristocratic solitude; and Emmet, for his courageous idealism.

Yeats, when his efforts to spread propaganda for the nationalist cause seemed to accomplish little, became greatly discouraged. He wondered whether the fires of patriotism were but sad dying embers; hence he was moved to deplore what he considered the reason for this apathy: the increasing interest of the people of a changing Ireland in money making had dulled the ardor of their fighting spirit. The heroic reawakening of Ireland in the Easter Week Rebellion in 1916, of course, demonstrated that he was wrong.

The spirit of Yeats can be felt breathing freely through the three political dramas—*Patriots, The Dreamers, The Lost Leader* —that Robinson wrote between 1911 and 1918, for each play presents a study of either Yeats's political views or his national heroes. Through their similar background of the Irish political scene at various important stages in its advance to freedom, the plays fit into a common frame.

Patriots, the first of these, was written slowly when the playwright was traveling with the Abbey Company on its maiden visit to America, and was first produced by him at the Abbey on April 11, 1912. The finished script he read to some of the players for the first time while they were on a train bound for Chicago. In recollecting how he wrote *Patriots*, Robinson also went on to explain his technique in playwriting:

> I seem to remember many early versions, drafts, scenarios, and I know that unless one is a dramatic genius this is the only sure method of playwriting: To write down your act scene by scene, numbering each scene in the manner of French plays making the entrance of each character the reason for a new scene, and jotting down only why the character has had to come in, what he has to say and what has to be said to him. But to write no word of dialogue until the scenes have been arranged to your satisfaction, until the bones of your sketch have fitted themselves to each other. The rest is almost child's play, for character

and dialogue shape themselves to the bones as inevitably as jelly shapes itself to its mould.[6]

For his theme in *Patriots* Robinson turns to the lack of patriotic fire in Ireland, already decried by Yeats; for his conflict, he sets in opposition the different political views motivating the young and the old generations in Ireland; for his background, he uses that narrow world of the small-town shopkeeper and not, as heretofore, the problems of the farming class. The struggle of the play is seen through the eyes of a physical-force revolutionary, James Nugent. Like Ellen in *The Cross Roads,* James prefers actions to words: "The soft way isn't the way to save Ireland, it's got to be the hard way, it's got to be the fighting way with rifle and sword."

Nugent comes home after being eighteen years in jail for a political murder, only to discover that the once intense and fighting patriotism of his friends and followers had softened into a complacent parliamentarianism. His tragedy begins when he attempts to revive their previous ardor. Inertia faces him on all sides and his oratorical powers, convincing in the olden days, make no impression on the townspeople. His relations and friends have other pursuits, while in the community at large pleasure seeking and profit making are paramount.

Even in his own home, his wife Anne, a capable and sincere but grasping woman, had lost her prior admiration for her husband's dreams. In the person of Anne, the playwright fashions a very competent character sketch, but he still shows some of his earlier bitterness in stressing the unpleasant traits of her nature. Anne now treats her husband as an interloper seeking to win away from her their only child, Rose, who has been crippled at birth through her father's neglect. Anne refuses to be reinspired regardless of her husband's plea:

James Nugent   Think of it Anne. Think of all the long weary years, the injustices that have been heaped upon us, the way we've been plundered of money, starved with famine, drained of our best blood, the crucified of nations. And think of it with the English driven out, a free country, a happy people, liberty at last.

Anne   Oh, don't talk to me of patriotism. I'm sick of it. It's made Sullivan a bankrupt; it's made Brennan a drunk and you a murderer; it's destroyed my happiness; it's made Rose a cripple.

Anne's fears about losing her daughter's affections are realized; the only ones responding to Nugent's appeals are the crippled Rose and her lover, Willie Sullivan, both stirred by a youthful zeal. With defeat staring him in the face, James Nugent determines to make one more fighting appeal to regain all his former allies to his standard. But he fails, for they are too caught up in pursuing their own egotistical ends. The only ones who come to the function at the local hall, where he hopes to turn the tide, are a couple of casual visitors, far more interested in knowing where the latest moving pictures are being held in the town than they are in attending a political gathering. This ironic touch was recommended by Lady Gregory, necessitating some revisions of Robinson's initial plot, since he had originally envisioned a successful ending to James Nugent's speech.

As the final curtain falls, there is again sharp irony in the climactic conclusion of Nugent's tragedy in his newly found world, although some implausibility arises in allowing one with such deep patriotic zeal as that shown by Nugent to give up so easily. Time and reality have now finally broken his spirit; only his former dreams give him slight and fleeting consolation:

I've killed a man, I've crippled a child. I got myself shut up for eighteen years. . . . I know I meant right and my prison cell used to be filled with sad faces of men like me who had given everything for Ireland— they wouldn't have come to me, would they, if I hadn't been of their company. They are here now—I see them all around me—there is Wolfe Tone and there is—Oh: quiet watching faces. I have tried—tried as you tried and been broken.

Later, when reexamining his play, Robinson evaluated with satisfaction its precise construction. His analysis implies, nevertheless, the somewhat mechanical nature of his use of balanced structure: "I like . . . the way each act ends—to use a musical analogy—on an unresolved chord . . . the situation which is to be the theme of the play does not appear till the act is two-thirds through, and then the characters on the stage and the audience are left in suspense—only in the sense of wondering what is going to happen next—suspense and surprise are surely two of the dramatist's sharpest darts." [7]

The handling of such a provocative subject as rebellion was a difficult one then for an Anglo-Irish writer in view of the increasing political tension in Ireland. In actuality, it anticipated by a year the tragedy of the Easter Rebellion in Dublin. But this play, as well as his other political ones, merited popular approval as sincere contributions to Irish political thought. More than that, to commemorate the first opening of the Dail Eireann, the Irish Parliament, by the Sinn Fein party on January 21, 1919, *Patriots*, significantly enough, was revived at the Abbey and received tremendous applause.[8]

III *Maturing as a Producer*

Because Robinson was under the spell of Ibsen, or in his words "Ibsen-foolish," he had managed at the very outset of his career as producer to persuade Yeats to allow him to direct *Little Eyolf*. Yeats consented only because he felt that here at least was one Ibsen play with something mystical about it. Robinson was almost half way through the preparatory direction when T. C. Murray submitted his *Birthright*, so Ibsen's play was put aside. Other plays from Seumas O'Kelly, Lady Gregory, Lord Dunsany, St. J. Ervine, Rutherford Mayne, Yeats, Douglas Hyde, William Boyle, Joseph Campbell, and from Robinson himself followed; and these admirably took care of the Abbey's needs. Finally, in 1913, Robinson satisfied his ambition to present plays of foreign authors; within a period of three months he produced dramas by Hauptmann, Strindberg, and Tagore.

About this time also Robinson was beginning to develop a very smooth working partnership with Yeats in directing plays. Miss Geraldine Cummins, who in 1952 wrote a biography of the Irish novelist, Dr. Edith Somerville, and for which Robinson wrote the preface, admiringly watched their teamwork at the Abbey during the rehearsals of one of her plays, *Broken Faith*, in 1913. In contrast to Lady Gregory, Robinson allowed her to be present during rehearsals. Recalling her experiences then, Miss Cummins writes that Robinson "accepted the useful suggestions made by Yeats for the intensification of a certain tragic situation. I, a silent witness, learnt then how two such fine minds working in harmony together can help bring out without overstressing the dramatic possibilities. The young inexperienced actors and actresses in this, the Second Company, admitted to me learning much from these two producers. When Robinson gave advice on construction, he was a man of few words but they were

all to the point. Unerringly he put his finger on the weak spots." [9]
Yeats kept a critically alert eye on Robinson's productions of
realistic plays. Thus, according to Robinson, after a performance
he could expect Yeats to make many criticisms: "I had hung the
pictures too high; the farmers' daughters were too clean (Smear
cow-dung on their faces! I remember him exclaiming), some
actor's wig was atrocious; the scene was too darkly lit." [10] Yeats
even became tired of the stage furniture: it was undistinguished.
Robinson then had to rummage with Yeats through old furniture
shops in Dublin, looking for genuine Georgian furniture. Yeats,
though, much impressed Robinson with the pains he took to make
sure that even the smallest prop was correct and with his eager-
ness to experiment with stagecraft. Robinson expressly appreci-
ated Yeats's interest in the specially designed scenes of Gordon
Craig for the Abbey.

Both men also liked to exchange views on the construction of
whatever play was being produced. On one occasion, they discussed where a playwright should best begin his rising action.
And Yeats became fascinated when Robinson mentioned that
Ibsen in the plays of his maturity moved towards a later and later
point of attack.

The two men, writes Walter Starkie, former director of the
Abbey, "of course, did not always agree on dramatic matters. I
always tried to back up Lennox, but I had a hard task with
Yeats who was against him at times." [11] One of Yeats's bones of
contention with Robinson was over the reading of poetic lines,
principally his own. But Robinson, Monk Gibbon adds, was
shrewd enough never to quarrel with Yeats about ideas.[12]

All the same, Robinson was sound vocally. Both Hilton Edwards and Shelah Richards, herself a noted actress and producer,
confirm this judgment based upon their observations of Robinson's
techniques as producer when he was at the height of his authority at the Abbey. Their reservations are directed rather against
his lack of skill in visualizing a performance. Edwards values
Robinson as "a past master in producing casts in the interpretation of their lines, now a lamentably neglected and all important
part of theatre craft." [13] Miss Richards agrees with her fellow
director about Robinson's key asset: "A false inflection would
never get past him. He had, though, a curiously blind eye for the
visual. The appearance of a play never seemed to affect him,

right or wrong. It often occurred to me that while he listened to a play—and the sound had to be right—he conjured the whole up in his mind and expected the audience to do the same." [14]

From the playwrights' point of view, some of them felt that Robinson would brook no rivals, that he could show an obvious streak of jealousy particularly if their plays showed promise. On the other hand, his custom of allowing them to attend his rehearsals of their plays and his kind understanding of their writing problems earned him their general respect and often their admiration. For example, Teresa Deevy, who came into prominence as an Abbey dramatist in the 1930's when the Abbey was still lively, writes in his praise: "He was always ready to listen to the author and to have the author beside him at rehearsal. Having said he liked to have an author beside him at rehearsal to be sure of giving the interpretation that was intended, he added, '*that* or *not* to come to any rehearsal, I can't tolerate last minute suggestions!' He never aimed to put his mark on the play (as some producers do) and therefore his mark was always on it." [15]

Robinson's harmonious relations with the players can be gathered from the tribute of one of Ireland's most brilliant actors, Micheál MacLiammoir, on the occasion of the Abbey Theatre Festival in 1938. "I have," he said, "always felt, that one of Lennox Robinson's unique qualities as an Irish dramatist is that, alone among his fellows in Dublin, with the possible exception of Denis Johnston, he understands the actor, has acted himself and knows our qualities and defects, our peculiarities and vanities, and jealousies and illusions, and all our funny little ways." [16]

Robinson in his dual capacity of playwright and producer reckoned the latter role as the more difficult; and, as for the poor actor, he was at the mercy of both. On one hand, speaking as a playwright, he thought that he should be in attendance at every rehearsal of his play, else his producer might completely misconceive important scenes in it and interpret them in a way he never intended.

On the other hand, in explaining his own light touch while directing actors, he showed discerning awareness of the problems facing any producer: "He can take very few liberties with the text of the play, a few lines cut here and there behind the author's back or with his grudging consent, . . . and in dealing with the players how delicately he must thread. Not because his in-

terference may be resented—the more experienced the player
the more he welcomes comment—but because his interference
may snuff out some new attitude or approach to character, some
new point of view, some fresh interpretation." [17]
On the third tour of the Abbey players to the United States in
the earlier part of 1914, Robinson once again joined them as
their manager. But war threatened, hence unlike the previous
two visits, this one failed to make a profit for the Company; and
the Abbey directors lost confidence in Robinson over his management policy. Lady Gregory especially was greatly disappointed
because she had looked forward to achieving financial freedom
for the Abbey through American aid. So she blamed Robinson
for unwisely choosing wrong places for their tour. Nonetheless,
the Irish plays and players from their visits, as Glen Hughes points
out, left seminal impressions upon young American writers, actors,
and directors.[18]
At the end of this tour, Robinson resigned from his position
with the theatre after being its most consistently successful
manager to date. He did so, he explained, "because after four
and a half years' ceaseless work there, I felt I had become stale
as a producer; production and management left me little time
for writing—It was hard to make ends meet and help my
family a little, for though players' salaries had quite rightly been
increased as the Theatre became more prosperous, mine still remained £150.—We parted with mutual consent and without un-
friendliness. . . . But though the break was my own choosing, it
was a wrench." [19]
Before returning to his home in West Cork, he spent some
weeks in London directing an Irish play at the Royal Court
Theatre and then visited Paris, his first trip to the Continent.
While at home, he wrote a new play and began work on a novel.
But the war and increasing political activity in Ireland caused
him to shelve temporarily his plans for the novel. Attracted to the
conservative nationalism of Redmond, he made up his mind to
answer Redmond's call for volunteers to fight with the Allies.
When it came to war, he believed that the Anglo-Irish ought to
act as their parents did for the sake of the Empire. He drilled
for six weeks with Redmond's Volunteers, but the War Office
would not recognize this special Irish division, and it soon dis-
banded. Next, he tried to enlist in the Munster Fusiliers, who

would not accept him because of his extreme nearsightedness. The remaining two months of 1914 he stayed at home, and, being jobless, he completely used up his savings. All he could afford was one cigarette a day.

IV   The Dreamers

In the beginning of 1915 Robinson returned to Dublin where he lived at the home of Mrs. Hester Travers-Smith, the daughter of the eminent Irish scholar, Edward Dowden, and later Robinson's mother-in-law. A keen student of psychical phenomena, she eventually wrote a book, *Voices From the Void*, about them. Through her aid, Robinson obtained temporary employment in the filing division of the Teachers' Pension Fund. Meanwhile, he discussed plans with the new producer at the Abbey, A. P. Wilson, for the opening night of his latest play, *The Dreamers*, on February 10. In the cast was Barry Fitzgerald, who was acting his first part.

Robinson in *The Dreamers* goes back to an earlier period in Irish political history, centering his attention on the frustrated deeds of the young insurrectionist Robert Emmet. The quixotic yet heroic sacrifice of Emmet, in the very nature of its romantic and tragic circumstances, pulsed with drama. Thomas Moore had already spread his dead friend's fame through his poignant verses; and Yeats, faithful to Emmet's memory, had used the idealistic hero's story in his American lectures to promote the Irish nationalist cause there.

The same hero also inspired Robinson. In his preface to the play he mentions how he will deal with events of history: "There is fact in this play and there is fancy and only the student of those dreaming days will know where the one merges with the other." For all those who might quarrel with his title and his play, Robinson incorporates a sense of dreamy idealism in his defense: "Emmet was practical in all his qualities, a soldier, a tactician, a most able organizer, I agree. But all these things were fused together for one purpose by the most practical quality of all—his dream. Dreams are the only permanent things in life, the only heritage that can be hoarded or spent, and yet handed down intact from generation to generation. Robert Emmet's dream came down to him through—how many?—generations. He passed it on undimmed. It is being dreamed to-day; as vivid as ever and they say as unpractical." [20]

The playwright concentrates on the period between July 16 and July 23, 1803, when Emmet's rebellion against English control in Ireland tragically failed. To this historical fact he joins the romance of Emmet and Sarah Curran. To give full historical veracity to his story, the author crowds his stage with characters; so much so that, despite the technical ability he displays in handling such a number of people, he fails to give a full portrayal of any one individual. One accordingly gets the impression of vagueness in characterization; the characters seem to hide their true innerselves.

The two lovers are made to appear the victims of the people's lack of spirit and cooperation in the uprising, and Emmet's followers spend their time either drinking or quarreling. Actually, on the opening night, although the play as a whole was well received, the scene showing the crowd carousing and squabbling among themselves at the White Bull Inn aroused hissing and laughter among the Abbey audience.[21]

Most of the emphasis in *The Dreamers* lies in the tragic side of the frustrated objectives of the enthusiastic dreamer. At the end, defeated and disheartened, Emmet seeks some consolation in the womanly understanding of Sarah:

Sarah   There was everything in it, Robert, truth, freedom, justice. . . .

Emmet   Yes, yes, of course there was . . . and murder, Oh, Sarah, truth and justice seemed far away. All was so different to what I had expected. If I could have died the sword in hand. . . .

Sarah   Please God, you've been spared to wipe out and atone for that unfortunate night's work.

Emmet   Ah, if I only could! If now I were to disappear for ever I know how lightly men without candour will pronounce on this failure without knowing one of the circumstances that occasioned it. They will consider only that they predicted it. They will not recollect that they predicted also that no preparations could be made—that no plan could be conceived—that no day could be fixed without being instantly known to the Castle. All this I did but they will never be just enough to acknowledge it. Oh, if I were to die to-morrow all I would ask from the world would be the charity of its silence.

Emmet's life thus dramatizes a favorite subject of the playwright: the conflict of the dreamer and of the idealist with reality. In retrospect, one notes that reality has brought tragedy or disillusionment to all Robinson's dreamers: Nugent's ideals are blocked, and he is left alone to carry on his fight for his dreams; Ellen's hopes for better conditions for her community are mere mocking fantasies; Mary, the kept woman, learns only too soon that her romantic ideas of the simple life on the farm are only illusions. But, in spite of these setbacks, the dreamers can, after all, be sources of inspiration in the realm of the here and now. Although their efforts may be abortive, their ideals can be a guiding light to those who follow after them. Are not dreams, after all, "the only permanent thing in life, the only heritage that can be hoarded or spent and yet handed down intact from generation to generation."

V Applied Nationalism

At the time that Robinson came to stay with Mrs. Travers-Smith, séances were all the rage among the literati in Dublin. Not surprisingly Mrs. Travers-Smith's interest in spiritualism prompted her to form a séance circle that met several times each week in her home. She was also reported in the London *Daily News* to have made contact with Oscar Wilde during one of her automatic-writing experiments. From the spirit world the writing brought forth Wilde's caustic messages on living authors. When asked what he thought of George Moore, the reply came, "My little countryman from Dublin! Little Moore is absolutely little in mind and soul. Moore is a dwarf and thinks himself a giant." [22]

Mrs. Smith's encouragement led Robinson to take part in the activities of her spiritualistic meetings: "My psychic powers were small, but I seemed to add strength to the sittings and her great powers developed enormously. Communications came sometimes by automatic writing but chiefly by ouija board. . . . After months of working together the replies to questions came with extraordinary rapidity and clearness. . . ." [23]

Robinson later abandoned spiritualism; but, as his writing reveals, he retained interest in the strangeness of the preternatural and in the psychic phenomena of the spirit world. At one time, for instance, he attempted writing a murder play which had spiritualism as its subject, but he never completed it. Being good at fortunetelling with cards, he liked telling either his own or that of others; and often to amuse himself he would check on his horoscope in the newspapers.

His work with the Teachers' Pension Office lasted only a few months, and then he moved to a more satisfactory but equally short-lived post with the Paymaster-General's Office in Dublin Castle. In the summer of 1915, Sir Horace Plunkett offered him a more permanent assignment as an Organizing Librarian in the southeast of Ireland for the Carnegie Trust at a salary of £150 a year. Sir Horace, after ranching for ten years in the United States to restore his health, had come back to Ireland eager to contribute to the Irish cause and to revivify farming life there through cooperative societies. His practical nationalistic creed, with which Robinson sympathized, was based on better farming for better business for better living. And better rural libraries were needed for better living.

The greater part of Robinson's new task centered in the revival of derelict libraries in Limerick and Kerry and the supervision of new building construction in these counties. His organizing work brought him to West Limerick, where he knew slightly the Dermod O'Briens of Cahirmoyle near the Shannon River. Along with being a distinguished portrait painter and long-time president of the Royal Hibernian Academy, O'Brien also tried to farm the six hundred acres on his estate. Robinson, in 1948, wrote an admiring biography of him, entitled *Palette and Plough,* which dealt with his career as a painter and as a generous, sympathetic landlord.

Because Robinson was a protégé of their friend, Sir Horace Plunkett, the O'Briens invited him to stay at their large Italianate country house, looking towards the rich farmlands of the Golden Vale. He arrived at lunch time with a young inspector from the Department of Agriculture who had come down from Dublin to talk to Mrs. O'Brien about her special breed of hairless puck goats. One of them had died suddenly of a mysterious disease, and she had sent the carcass to a professor at the Agricultural College in Dublin for examination. The professor was tardy about his report. At last he replied, apologizing profusely for his oversight in not thanking her earlier for the gift of a venison which his family and he had greatly enjoyed eating. Over lunch, Mrs.

O'Brien confused the identity of her guests and talked to Robinson about puck goats and to the agricultural inspector about libraries. Robinson was not to forget this episode, for in his best comedy, *The Whiteheaded Boy,* Aunt Ellen, who is modeled after Mrs. O'Brien, "keeps queer outlandish goats."

While a library organizer, Robinson spent busy mornings and afternoons splashing through rain puddles on bumpy, muddy country roads as he rode on his motorcycle nicknamed by some "Dash," by others "Prudence." Evenings at Cahirmoyle meant that he had to dress for dinner in dinner jacket and black tie. Then all adjourned afterwards to the lamp-lit library, where, seated around the fireside, they frequently played classical trio music for cello, violin, and piano. One winter Mrs. O'Brien taught Robinson her beloved Dante which she knew almost by heart. His host, moreover, had Robinson pose for two portraits: one showed him reading a book with a cat on his knee; the other playing a violin, the instrument almost covered by his immensely long fingers. Both of these were displayed at the Exhibition of the Royal Hibernian Academy in 1918.

Robinson's experiences as an organizer for the Carnegie Trust gave him some of the most enjoyable years of his life. It permitted him to make friendly ties with all kinds of country and small-town people from every walk of life and thus to view the Irish scene with enlarged understanding, with greater maturity. Although there were quite a few petty rows, Robinson, on the whole, managed to win the cooperation of those desirous of furthering the cultural life of their community. On his rounds, Robinson could record with approval the spread of the Sinn Fein movement for Irish political freedom. He made this report to Sir Horace in Dublin: "The first use that one restored library was put to was a meeting at which a splended energetic young priest—a tremendous Sinn Feiner, as are most of the young priests, sang rebel songs and enrolled 150 members. But we won't tell this to the other trustees." [24]

From the four years spent with the gracious, cultivated O'Briens, he gathered many indispensable impressions of Irish life that later became profitable sources of inspiration to him in his plays. As well, their sympathetic awareness of his needs as a writer stimulated him to create two of the most artistically successful of his works: *The Lost Leader* and *The Whiteheaded Boy.*

VI *Nationalist Non-Dramatic Writings*

The evolution of Robinson's nationalism, which he perforce tailored to fit his background and upbringing, is more clearly and fully brought into focus in his two prose works published in Dublin within a year of each other. The first of these is his fictional autobiography, *A Young Man from the South,* published in 1917. This, his only novel, presents a slight but sympathetically delineated study of its hero, Willie Powell, as viewed through the eyes of three of his former Dublin friends for the benefit of an inquiring English visitor.

In his foreword written in July, 1916, Robinson traced the growth of his novel. He began it in the autumn of 1914, put it aside for a year, and completed it on New Year's Eve, 1916. He then sent it to a publishing house in Dublin, but its offices were burned during the Easter Week Rebellion and his manuscript was destroyed.

Consequently, he had to rewrite his book with the aid of a jumbled alternate manuscript. While doing so, the relevance of his material to the Rebellion and its tragic aftermath almost made him adjust his material to agree with history. But then, on reflection, he felt the changes would do more harm than good, so he kept to his original purpose of revealing an important aspect of the Irish mind and feeling. However, he pointed out that—if he had rewritten the manuscript—its hero, Willie, would have been found fighting by the side of the slain leaders in the rebellion.

Willie is a young Anglo-Irishman from Southwest Cork with Protestant and unionist leanings. He is slightly melancholy; a perfect listener, but silent about himself; not very robust; and not very brilliant or clever. Though the least amorous of men, women think him sympathetic to them and want to protect him. Yeats's *Kathleen ni Houlihan* had made him patriotic, and now in Dublin he is attracted to the ideals of the Gaelic revival in literature and of the revolutionary Sinn Fein movement. He writes successful plays, their contents resemble those of Robinson's own; and he falls under the spell of the flamboyant and intensely patriotic Isabel Moore. In the climactic scene, the nationalists carry on an ignominious hand-to-hand fight with unionist college students and the police, causing Willie to feel ashamed of having joined with the balked nationalists. As a result, though Willie regrets nothing, his background induces him to doubt the strength of his nationalism; and he retires into obscurity to reappraise himself while rebuilding his patriotism on firmer grounds.

The novel today is helpful for the political, cultural, or social historian of Dublin and of Irish life in the early decades of this century. Robinson elucidates the relationship of the unionists to the nationalists, complains about the absence of adequate critical standards in the arts, and throws light on the psychology behind the 1916 Easter Rebellion. Many of the novel's characters, too, bear a close likeness to well-known personalities in the Irish capital at that time: Isabel Moore, for instance, is based on Countess Markievicz; Maurice Damer, on Padraic Pearse; and Bennett, on George Russell.

Robinson's political concerns were also set forth in a collection of four brief sketches published in 1918. Because of the mournful aftermath of the dramatic Easter Rebellion, he entitled this volume *Dark Days*. These pieces were penned between August, 1915, and August, 1916; two of them, "An Irishwoman" and "A Sinn Feiner," first appeared in *The New Statesman*.

In *Dark Days* Robinson discloses his mental and emotional adjustment to current political events. Two of his sketches, "A Sinn Feiner" and "In Silence and Tears"—one written a month after "The Rising" and the other three months later—best exemplify the salient features and boundaries of his nationalism.

His "Sinn Feiner" character harked back to the time he acquired a sense of intense dedication from his love of country. His idealized image of Ireland soon assumed the proportions of being a new religion. As a matter of fact, in the life of this "Sinn Feiner" "religion in the ordinary sense, as he grew older, receded farther from him, it touched him less and less; knowing his own weakness, he is glad of that image he raised (false God though many call it), he knows it has kept him cleaner, straighter, truer." [25] His work, although allied to his ideal, did not allow him to join himself fully with the Sinn Fein party. He also stayed apart because he did not agree with its means for achieving freedom, because he believed the members to have been "madly mistaken," to have "done to death the thing they and he loved." Perhaps a less bloody means might be used to gain independence. But his sorrow at the death of Pearse and the other leaders, all of whom he revered for their dreams, has led him—much like "The Young Man from the South"—to reexamine his heart for some weakness that kept him aloof.

In "Silence and Tears" Robinson paid respect to the memory of Sir Roger Casement, who had just been hanged as a traitor in England in August, 1916. At the same time, Robinson proclaimed that the Sinn Fein Rising was "the biggest moving force in Ireland since the Young Ireland of the forties," "the beginning of a new epoch." The impact of Casement's death upon him hit home, when shortly afterwards he attended one of Boucicault's trite melodramas with some friends. During the performance the entire audience rose to join the actors in singing with tremendous and passionate intensity the play's mournful refrain, "For they're hangin' men and women there for wearin' o the green."

VII   The Lost Leader

The third and last of Robinson's political plays, *The Lost Leader*, received its premiere at the Abbey on February 19, 1918, before a packed and very attentive house. In session then in Dublin was the Home Rule Convention, which Lloyd George had called the previous year; it had as its general chairman Sir Horace Plunkett through whom Robinson was appointed secretary for one of the committees. Accordingly it was rumored in Dublin that Robinson had specially written *The Lost Leader* to help his sponsor make a success of the Convention. Prior to the play's production, Robinson, at Yeats's advice, made some changes with the aid of Dr. Gogarty, in an attempt to strengthen the play's ending.

All the same, the report of the diarist, Joseph Holloway indicates that the tinkering on the last act was not quite successful. In his opinion, "Act I was arresting; Act II continued more or less so and Act III halted somewhat, and the tragic death scene was slightly marred by the prolonged delay in dropping the curtain. But the whole thing struck me as a big achievement. It is undoubtedly the most ambitious political play yet presented to the public." [26]

In *The Lost Leader*, Robinson unfolds what William Archer praised as "one of the most imaginative plays of our time." [27] One evening, while Robinson was walking down Merrion Square in Dublin, the idea struck him that the nearness of Parnell's death could make the possibility of the Irish leader being still alive an excellent subject for a drama. He began to ruminate: suppose Parnell had not died in 1891 at all; suppose his coffin really contained, as many imagined, the body of an unknown Russian immigrant; suppose he were still alive, then how would he act? Three days after such speculation Robinson had finished his drama.

With such an air of romantic wondering about reality, Robinson enters into the story of his play. An old man, Lucius Lenihan, has hidden himself in some remote corner of the west of Ireland, where he is part owner of the only hotel in the village. Into this quiet scene, on an October afternoon in 1917, come three men; a psychiatrist, his friend, and an international journalist eagerly seeking a human interest story. The doctor learns that Lucius has been suffering from bad dreams; and, after discussing the psychology of the case with his friend, he asserts that hypnosis will cure Lucius. He then sends Lucius into a trance; and, while in this state, Lucius gives the impression that he is Parnell. But the author does not leave his audience fully certain about this. The doubt is further intensified in the second act when, in the excitement of the possibility of Parnell's being alive, Mary, niece of Lucius, tells the doctor that her uncle once suffered from the delusion that he was Parnell. Only after Parnell's death was Lucius cured of his mental sickness; living a quiet life aids him to retain his sanity.

The author counterbalances this by allowing Lucius to explain how his brother had kept him alive, even though everyone thought he was dead. Thus he speaks as a resurrected Parnell with the belief that he has a mission and that his enforced silence must be broken. He can no longer live in peace in view of Ireland's needs. He loves Ireland, and none of the present leaders are sufficiently competent to save her; they are neither forceful enough for the great tasks ahead nor clever enough to develop satisfactory plans. The country in its present state will be lost without him. The doctor, still skeptical, decides to wait until the arrival of some former followers of Parnell, who have been summoned to identify Lucius.

In the third act, to fill in pending the arrival of the witnesses,

The Romantic in Politics

Robinson summarizes Ireland's political conflicts. Three parties receive the limelight: Sinn Fein, Unionist, and the United Irish League. Of these, the last group fares the worst. Its representative is revealed as spineless and as lacking initiative; his thoughts are not his own, for the local monsignor forms them. The spiritual side of Sinn Fein, however, receives Robinson's approval. In a telling theatrical finale, Lucius moves to the top of a nearby hill and with the sunset glowing behind him delivers his saving message for his countrymen. While the various political views are bandied about, Lucius, using the actual words of Parnell, continues to expound loftily on his ideals for unification of all parties in a common cause. In the person of Long John Flavin, a cunning local shopkeeper, who had great distaste for Parnell's views, Robinson—just as Yeats did before him—tilts at the "Gombeen" men. Flavin scorns Lucius's appeal to unite for freedom under a spiritual banner:

Lucius   I can sweep Ireland by appealing to her soul . . . . I learnt long ago . . . that to catch and move men you must appeal to their desires, you must rouse their passion for riches, passion for justice, selfish passions, unselfish passions. But now I feel there is in Ireland a vague passion, an objectless desire. It's the great moment that comes but once or twice in a nation's history, it's when the water stirs, it's when the mind of a nation is broken up, is ready to be moulded, is soft clay, warm wax. That moment has come now. . . . On my statue you wrote my words, that no bounds could be set to the progress of a nation, and will you erect a boundary to the progress of a human soul? Will you erect a boundary to the progress of a nation's soul. . . ?

Long John   If you'd tried that talk long ago, they'd have sent you packing.

Lucius   Yes, we couldn't have spirituality in the eighties, we had to be materialists. What's the use of preaching spirituality to an empty belly? . . . But don't think that even then I didn't realize dimly that there still remained this greater fight, a fight for the possession of a nation's soul. . . . Each year that passed made that battle more necessary, for each year Ireland grew more prosperous and more dead until Home Rule became merely the exchange of government by English shopkeepers for government by Irish gombeen men. . . . I understand that no nation can live by bread alone, that a nation must be noble and beautiful before it can be free—spiritually; that we must recognize that our battle cries are only symbols and that when we speak of parliaments and republics we speak of shadows of a shadow. . . . And those shadows I shall scatter.

Houlihan, an old blind tramp, who firmly believes Lucius to be Parnell, cannot bear any longer the niggling remarks of Long John against Lucius. He rises in anger at Long John's skepticism and tries to strike him with a hurley stick. The blow misses Long John, and Lucius is killed instead. Yet, when the witnesses arrive to test Parnell's identity, one is still left wondering. The man lying dead before them has a strong likeness to Parnell, though they are not sure. Perhaps he is the "Lost Leader"; perhaps he is not. The play thus ends on a questioning note:

Powell-Harper   Ah, you believe in Ireland?

Mary   I believe in God.

Houlihan   (Lifting his head) Let you go down on your knees all of you, his spirit is passing. He's leaving us, we're lost. . . . May God have mercy on his soul; may he have pity on Ireland. [It has grown very dark, there goes a sudden gust of wind and a splash of rain. The ray from the lamp shines steadily on the dead face. The eyes are closed, the lines of suffering, of indignation, of scorn, have been smoothed away. A great dignity and peace brood over the face of Lucius Lenihan or is it the face of Charles Stuart Parnell?]

In *The Lost Leader* one can discern intimations of Robinson's later attraction to the symbolistic, the psychic, and the speculative elements in literature. He covers his play with an air of mystery, the mystery that lies behind reality. In his preface, which echoes the voice of Yeats, he prepares one for this atmosphere: "Our battles are only symbols, and parliaments and republics are shadows of a shadow and in the storms and darkness amid tragedy, hate, disaster, and death I clasp Mary Lenihan's hand. For I, like her, believe in Ireland and in God."

The play's principal defect lies in its lack of unity of purpose which causes some confusion in interpretation. Did the author have a tragedy in mind? Did he think of it as tragi-comedy? Did he regard it as essentially symbolistic drama? If he meant the play to be a tragedy, the nature of the death of the central character prevents it from becoming one. Lucius, who is a well-etched character, meets his end by a conveniently accidental death. If the playwright meant tragi-comedy, the comedy is sporadic and slight; and the comic squabbling of the politicians in the third act leads to the accidential blow that kills Lucius. Even on the higher plane of symbolism, the play fails; for again the accidental death mars such a potential interpretation.

The considerable merits of *The Lost Leader,* nonetheless, won the plaudits of various literary celebrities. Galsworthy, Yeats, and George Moore were among those sending words of high praise and encouragement for the playwright's most successful work to date. Galsworthy applauded "The almost perfection of the first act";[28] and Yeats's short note of approval from Broad Street, Oxford, displayed his absentmindedness: "I now find that I put your telephone for an address. I hope it [the letter] has reached you. I think your play exceedingly remarkable, probably the best work you have done." [29]

Writing from 121 Ebury Street, London, Moore mingled commendation and criticism in his evaluation of *The Lost Leader:*

Your play, *A Lost Leader,* provides me with the pleasure of writing to an author to tell him that I wholly appreciate his work, and look upon it as a work of art. A masterpiece, your play is certainly among modern plays, and I have hardly a fault to find anywhere. . . . In the second act you carry the play nearly into a wrong key but the ballad singer saves you and you get back to your key. . . . The only fault I have to find is a certain inadequacy in the "Lost Leader's" utterance. Spiritual influence is a phrase that means hardly anything and it seemed to me that your wings wearied and fluttered now and then; and again almost helplessly in the last act when you speak of a spiritual sacrifice. To admire a play throughout except for a few utterances in the second act and a dozen more in the third act is a very unusual experience in my life. I am very grateful to you for it.[30]

One can observe two noteworthy patterns in Robinson's works up to now. First, there comes more clearly to light an underlying romantic strain in the playwright's nature. Previously it was submerged under his realism, but brief glimpses of it could be seen in his portrayal of Ellen in *The Cross Roads* and of Mary in *Harvest.* This characteristic of his finds expression in his use of what becomes in time his favorite theme: the dreamer's response to the realities of life. The catharsis he achieves in giving rein to his "romantic realism" can account in part for the progressive elimination of the sour note marring the atmosphere of his plays up to this point. One need but examine *The Lost Leader* to realize how much more sympathetic he has become toward his characters; here for the first time he has erased his familiar pessimistic tone. Parallel to this trend, there is also discernible an increasing objectivity: he replaces his propensity for reforming didacticism, as manifested in *The Cross Roads* and *Harvest,* with a sense of relaxed detachment in his handling of his literary creations. At this stage in his life he could aptly state that he now had "an unfortunate habit of seeing my friends' faults as clearly as my enemies' faults. . . ."[31]

CHAPTER 4

The Mellowed Mood

THIS next phase of Robinson's literary development can be considered as quite an important one for him because of the gains he derives from his changed attitude while manipulating his dramatic ingredients. He gave evidence of his growing maturity in *The Lost Leader*, where time, taste, and experience were exerting a corrective influence in softening the acerbity of his earlier outlook. This mellowing process comes to a head in his plays during this period. He now smilingly enjoys the children of his imagination instead of prodding them with ironically bitter barbs. The comic spirit is in the ascendant, and the playwright welcomes it openly and fully.

By its nature, comedy works differently from tragedy to achieve its effects. To a great extent, it presupposes the existence of a friendly, playful mood and the ability to adopt an air of reflective detachment towards the subject. This frame of mind, in turn, allows one to perceive more clearly the incongruity existing between idea and fact, which Schopenhauer claimed to be the greatest source of laughter. Generally speaking, the best comedies in the theatre seem to derive their comic substance from the absurdities that arise in comparing the normal with the "non-normal." One can also observe in these comedies at least one character, who, while carefully individualized, is set forth as free from any flaws of personality. Such a person acts as a foil for the odd types, the deviations from the norm; and he also enhances their peculiarities. This source of the comic, in particular, Robinson frequently uses in his comedies of Irish life.

Strangely enough the Irish theatre, on the whole, seems rather deficient in comedy, although it is chiefly rich in farce. This lack is all the more surprising when one considers that the Irishman is known to the outside world for his humorous, devil-may-care outlook on life and for being reasonably free from the bourgeois smugness so antipathetic to comedy. Close to home, though, it would seem that the nature of the Irishman functions differently. In a nation where religion is the dominant reality, the Irishman seems more predisposed toward that note of high seriousness characterizing tragedy. This moral earnestness brings with it an urge for moral uplift; whenever, therefore, the comic spirit arises in Ireland, the Irish writer is generally prone to poke fun at conditions to improve them.

I   The Whiteheaded Boy

The humor scattered here and there throughout Robinson's earlier pessimistic plays at least gave testimony that he was quite conscious of laughable human defects. But with the presentation at the Abbey on December 13, 1916, of *The Whiteheaded Boy*, his first full-length comedy, Robinson emerged as a comic writer of stature. In fact over the years, this, his most successful play, gained for him an international reputation, being translated into various languages.

Because *The Whiteheaded Boy* came between two political plays, *The Dreamers* and *The Lost Leader*, Robinson regarded it also as political in intent. The allegory, nevertheless, is very brief and even inconsistent; for this reason it seems far more desirable to consider his play as a superb comedy of Irish family life, as a classic of its kind.

Robinson dedicated his comedy to Mrs. Dermod O'Brien of Cahirmoyle, calling her "Aunt Ellen." Something of the background attached to Robinson's play is described in his memories of his stay with the O'Brien family: "Two years after *The Dreamers,* I was to make a more successful effort. I begged an hour of Dermod O'Brien's time and outlined the plot of a comedy and asked him did he think there was the makings of a play in it. He thought there was, and in one week I wrote it in three acts, and rewrote them the next week, and it was accepted by Mr. Yeats but without enthusiasm. Those fourteen days work were to bring me many thousands of pounds as the years went on." [1]

Mrs. Brigid Ganly, the noted Irish artist and the daughter of the O'Briens, recollects that Robinson, just after he had finished typing his manuscript for *The Whiteheaded Boy,* came to her mother and asked her permission to read his play to the assembled family:

We were all agog, but remembering the unrelieved gloom of "The Lost Leader" and "Harvest" we composed our features with proper gravity. But as the reading of "The Whiteheaded Boy" proceeded, irresistible laughter took hold of the delighted audience. Sayings culled by my mother from her visits to the cottages were recognized: "The menagerie of the Geoghans!" [Geoghegan in the play] Even the hairless goat. And was there not a faint flavour of my mother's endless efforts at improving the lives of the villagers, to be found in Aunt Ellen and her wonderful schemes. At the play on the opening night the original Mrs. Geoghan wept, and said, "My heart's broke!" [2]

As with nearly all Irish comedies, *The Whiteheaded Boy* is satirical in purpose, illustrating many of the foibles of Irish character. Robinson good humoredly directs his satire against faulty upbringing of children and against those who expect that education will make a silk purse out of a sow's ear. The same idea was also found in *Harvest,* but there the theme was obliterated in the family tragedy.

The play ripples along gaily with not a syllable out of place; the action of its plot emerges automatically from the psychology of the characters. In its perfection of dramatic economy, there are not many comedies to rival it on the contemporary stage. Actually, Michael Dolan, while directing the first production of O'Casey's comedy, *Nannie's Night Out,* at the Abbey, recommended *The Whiteheaded Boy* to him as a model because it seized and built up interest from the rise of the curtain.

Entering, as it were, into the spirit of the occasion, Robinson expands his customary simple stage directions into narrative form; in this unusual and pleasing way he is able to act as a commentator on his characters' little frailties and to set the gay insouciant mood of the comedy. He begins his play:

Mrs. Geoghegan's house is at the head of the street, facing the priest's house; the shop is at the other end of the village, between Michael Brosnan's public-house and Duffy's yard. William Geoghegan (God rest his soul) was a very genteel man, and when his wife brought him the house and the bit of land, instead of getting a tenant for it like a reasonable man (and the whole village knew Clancy, the vet., was mad to take it) nothing would do him but live in it himself and walk down to business every day like a millionaire. 'Tis too high notions poor William always had and his sister, Ellen, worse again than himself, craning after anything new. She'd be like a cow through a fence—but indeed William's notions didn't stand too well with him, and when he died he left six of them no less in a poor enough way. . . .

You're admiring the furniture? 'Twas got five years ago at the Major's auction. A big price they had to pay for it too, George didn't want to buy it but the mother's heart was set on it. They got new horse hair put in the arm chair, the Major had it wore to the wood sitting all day over the fire; cursing the government and drinking whiskey.

Aren't the pictures lovely? They're all enlarged photographs of William's family. . . . They're after setting the tea; they got that lamp new this afternoon, isn't it giving a great light? Begob, there's a chicken and a shape and apples and a cake. —it must be the way they're expecting company.

Oh, the old one? That's Hannah. There's not a house in the village she hasn't been a servant in. She was at a hotel in Cork once. Two days they kept her.

Such is Robinson's setting for the comedy of situation that follows. In the Geoghegan family of six, there are three sons and three daughters. Denis, the youngest, is regarded by his adoring mother as the pride and pet of the family—"the whiteheaded boy." So Denis naturally receives all the privileges in the household, and the others are required to make sacrifices to enable Denis to obtain the education and treatment his mother believes should rightfully be his. She visualizes glowing prospects for his future. His medical studies at Trinity College should bring the family considerable social prestige later when he becomes a doctor. But Denis has other plans.

In gay fashion Denis finds more time for studying the racing form rather than the human form. Consequently, he fails his medical examinations for a third time. When the telegram comes to the Geoghegan family announcing his latest failure, it is inadvertently opened; and the other children, on hearing the result, agree to stand no more of Denis's nonsense. But the mother is not set back by this. She cannot possibly conceive of anything being wrong; in truth, since the day of his birth, she has always felt he was different from the others.

The Mellowed Mood

"The whiteheaded boy" after his arrival home faces growing discontent in the family against his reign. But this does not disturb him; worse still, he expects to continue in his favored role. The family then rebels: it is time that some of the others have a chance. "Baby," a woman now close on thirty, wants to train in Dublin as a secretary; Jane wishes to marry but without an adequate dowry she cannot; and Peter, who is anxious to seek for a better job out of town, lacks the money to leave home and begin his search. Hence, as the head of the household, George, the oldest boy, determines to correct matters. Denis had better take a gift of money from the family and try his luck in Canada.

But Denis is a man of spirit and independence. He points out quite truly that he never desired to become a doctor. They all told him that he was clever; and now that they have found out otherwise, they want to blame him for their false estimate of him and for their misguided ambitions.

Denis, engaged to Delia Duffy, realizes that a rough-and-tumble life in Canada will not be good enough for his future wife and writes her a note calling off their engagement. From then on, he has the family completely in his control. Delia's father, thinking that his prestige in town will suffer, rushes in on the family and hurls all kinds of threats at the trembling Geoghegans. At this point, Aunt Ellen, a well-to-do relation, whom the Geoghegan family foster for her money, resolves to rescue the family from being sued. Thereupon ensues what is easily the best of Robinson's comedy love scenes. Here are the two elderly lovers:

Duffy is one of the solidest men in Ballycolman, Chairman of the District Council, Chairman of the Race committee and a member of every Committee and every League in the village. He has three public houses and a grocery business and the Post Office and a branch of the National Bank once a month, and a trade in old hens and eggs, and a terrible turnover in turkeys at Christmas. Oh, a weighty man—yes, he buried his wife long ago. . . .

Here's Ellen Geoghegan herself along with Jane. You could tell from her appearance the sort she is, a bit cranky and a nasty twist to her tongue if she liked, full of notions and schemes, she's a terrible one for reading; 'tis that has her head turned; there's not a week she hasn't the "Free Press," the "Eagle" and the supplement to the "Examiner" read to the bone. Still and all, she's a woman to be respected, she must have a couple of hundred acres back there at Kilmurray, and 'tis she owns them three small-houses at the other end of the village. . . . Yes, indeed, a wonder she never married—too many notions maybe.

Duffy tells Aunt Ellen that if she will marry him and give him £100, he will not trouble the family anymore.

Aunt Ellen   I couldn't John, I'm old, I'd like to be free.

Duffy   Goodnight, so.

Aunt Ellen   Why are you going?

Duffy   What is the use in me staying?

Aunt Ellen   What about the case?

Duffy   I'll see the lawyer in the morning.

Aunt Ellen   You're a hard man. You always get what you want.

Duffy   I didn't get the one thing I wanted in all the world.

The love battle between them gathers momentum as Duffy's courage increases. So he spurns Aunt Ellen's offer of money because she will not also promise to marry him. She asks why is he so persistent.

Duffy   Contrariness I suppose (He's kissed her, glory be to God!). . . .

Aunt Ellen   You're a terrible man.

Duffy   Why the devil didn't you let me do that thirty years ago, when we were boy and girl together? I made an offer of it one time, and you slapped me across the face.

Aunt Ellen   It's what I'd like to do to you this minute.

Duffy   You may then (Look at him sticking his face out to her.)

Aunt Ellen   Get along with you!

Duffy   Cripes! I'd like to get drunk. I'd like to pull the house down, I'd like to go bawling, singing through the streets of Ballycolman. . . . I'm twenty years old, not a minute more. Faith that reminds me. I'll draw up another paper and you can sign it. (He's always an eye to business). . . .

The Mellowed Mood

Aunt Ellen For the love of goodness, don't breathe a word of this to the Geoghegans. They'd have my life for making terms with you.

Duffy I'll not open my lips. Isn't it like a story in the pictures, Ellen, the way you and I have come together at the end of all. (*More love-making. Look at his arm round her waist.*)

Aunt Ellen Leave go of me; there's someone coming. (*It's George. She's all a flutter and no wonder.*)

Meanwhile, unknown to all, Denis and Delia resolve to marry. To support his wife and himself, he then settles on working as an unskilled laborer. But when the others hear about Denis's declaration of independence, rather than let him remain in such a job and ruin the social standing of both families in the town, all promise to do anything for the newlyweds. Duffy then offers Denis and his wife a store and a chance to go their own way. John Duffy says: "Free? Bedad, isn't he like old Ireland asking for freedom, and we're like the fools of Englishmen offering him every bloody thing except the one thing? So Denis, do like a darling boy; go out to Kilmurray and manage the shop."

These lines, Robinson felt, give the clue to the political allegory in the play. He is thereby attempting to satirize the position of Ireland as a family member of the British Empire. While Denis—as Ireland—wants to be free to live life his own way, George, the head of the house—as England—assumes that well-intentioned financial support should be enough for him.

Finally, Duffy wins a marriage promise from Aunt Ellen, when he tells her that he will try to improve her farm which she plans to will to Denis and Delia:

Aunt Ellen Girls look here. I've a plan in my mind for you all. After I'm married.

All After you're what?
> (*They think she's mad*)

Duffy After we're married.

Baby That's the boldest plan she ever made. After you're married! Wisha God help you John Duffy.
> (*And she's right*)

[93]

Thus has Robinson treated his characters, whom, in his earlier days, he would have handled with stinging irony. Very apt was Lady Gregory's comment that he had waded through streams of blood to *The Whiteheaded Boy.* Robinson's youthful pessimism masked the fact that he was more optimistic about life and people than he cared to concede. His changed view of life now gives him a suitably fresh vista on his characters—a vista charmingly whimsical and gay.

II *Troubled Years*

Promotion to the Advisory Committee on the Carnegie Library Trust came Robinson's way in 1919 after his years of field work. Since this position required frequent visits to the Trust's headquarters in Dublin, he saw less and less of the O'Brien's at Cahirmoyle. Meantime in Dublin, as an aftermath of the war, Yeats was faced with the breakdown of his hopes for a national theatre; actors especially were difficult to find to replace those lost during the war years. So Yeats, wanting to free himself from the responsibilities of the Abbey before moving to London, indicated through an intermediary that he was interested in having Robinson return as manager and producer, and that he should begin looking for players to rebuild the Company.

For financial reasons, though, Robinson wished to continue with his library post. And rather than resign he received permission from Sir Horace to remain as a committee member while directing at the Abbey. He pointed out in his letter to Sir Horace that as long as the Trust "pays me a small salary, they must be prepared for my trying to augment my income by working in my spare time for other people." [3]

Yeats, aware that the young were in the ascendancy in Irish life, argued with Lady Gregory on Robinson's behalf: "Lennox Robinson represents the Ireland that must sooner or later take the work from us; the sooner some young man, who feels that his own future is bound up with the Abbey is put in charge the better." [4] Lady Gregory, although showing the effects of her age, did not care to share her powers that easily. Besides, she still had not forgotten her criticisms of Robinson's handling of the third American tour. In her *Journals,* which Robinson edited in 1946, she recorded her objections to him. Among the personal faults she mentioned were his casualness, morbidity, and vagueness. But, she went on to add, "I don't want to fight and will try and work with him. It will be easier than working the Company myself, but I would have tried to do it." [5]

Robinson wanted a protective three-year contract; nevertheless, as her memoirs reveal, she persuaded him to accept less: "I had another talk with Robinson about his contract, saying that even in marriage settlements each side had for practical purposes to consider the other a rogue and that if he had to safeguard himself against capricious eviction, so had we in case he should take to drink or use the Theatre for the purposes Lord French is said to use the mansions he hires in London. So he gave into a year." [6] That, though, was not the end of her bargaining: "Later when I reflected, that there are now three blank months of the year which he would be doing nothing for us, it is hard that our low funds should give him £5 a week. And so when I arrived at the evening rehearsal, finding him alone I did the hardest thing first and spoke to him and he agreed to £2.10.0, so now all that unpleasant business is off my mind and I can work with him." [7]

Whatever later clashes of personality they may have had between them, they made, on the whole, an effective team. Each had qualities and gifts the other lacked, but together they courageously guided the Abbey through its sundry troubles. If he gave her suggestions for improving her plays, she helped him through the firmness of her managerial hand. Interestingly enough, her bedside books just before she died were the Bible and Robinson's edition of the *Golden Treasury of Irish Verse*.

Miss Elizabeth Coxhead, when preparing her biography of Lady Gregory, visited Robinson on his deathbed. She writes:

I thought he made a most beautiful figure out of the heroic literary past, lying there so long and thin, and talking in his soft, gently weary voice. I had the impression of a very sensitive and gifted person, quite without vanity and self importance and I came away much moved. I confined myself to the questions essential to me—had he helped with any of her plays besides *Damer's Gold* . . . . and then about his muddling things in America. "I expect I did muddle things," said Dr. Robinson with an infinitely rueful grace. He forebore to remind me he might well have done; that he was still a very young man at that time and ought not to have been given so much responsibility.[8]

Upon his return to the Abbey in April, 1919, Robinson set about reviving it, introducing a series of new plays most of which were very well received. Among his notable productions for that year were Lady Gregory's *The Dragon* with Barry Fitzgerald as the sleepy king enacting his first great role; Colum's *The Fiddler's House;* Corkery's *The Labour Leader;* Shaw's *Androcles and the Lion;* Gogarty's *The Enchanted Trousers;* and Yeats's *The Player Queen,* for which Robinson designed the scenery.

Shaw's play, after its opening performance on November 4, aroused an amusing controversy, which the *Evening Telegraph* in Dublin reported as "The Tailors and G.B.S." The Irish Branch of the Amalgamated Society of Tailors addressed an ungrammatical letter of protest to Robinson at the Abbey against Shaw's characterization of Androcles, the gentle, witty tailor: "At a special meeting held, the Abbey plays was discussed about the part of the tailor. The members think it is out of place and little making, and if you could remove it from the play they would feel obliged. An early reply will much oblige, and pardon me if I am intruding."

Robinson, who forwarded the letter to Shaw at 10 Adelphi Terrace, London, received this reply from him, dated November 13, 1919:

Thank you for sending me the letter of the _____ Tailors. I was amazed at its contents. Ever since the theatre existed tailors have been introduced into plays only to be ridiculed, called snip, made the butt of jests about being only the ninth part of a man, and represented as cowards and starvelings. Even Shakespeare makes the hero of one of his plays address a tailor in the following terms:

'Thou liest, thou thread, thou thimble,
Thou yard, three-quarters, half-yard, quarter, nail
Thou flea, thou nit, thou winter cricket thou. . . .

These lines have been spoken on the stage for three hundred years, and many others equally insulting by English authors and no Irish tailor has ever protested. But when I, an Irish author, for the first time, make a tailor the hero of a play, prepresenting him as gentle, kindly, brave, wise, devoted, a martyr to the Christian faith, and greatly the superior of the emperor, who runs to him for protection, then, if you please, for

the first time in history, a society of Irish tailors tells me that I am be-
littling them and asks me to remove the tailor from the play.

I shall feel much obliged if you will send copies of this correspondence
to the Amalgamated Society of Tailors, and ask them whether the views
of this branch represent the views of the whole society.

As I have been for forty years past a supporter of Labour and Trade
Unionism on the platform and in the Press, and have never put a play
on the stage in which the craft either of tailoring or any other form of
honourable labour was treated as a badge of inferiority, I am much surprised at being attacked in the quarter where I had the best right to
expect fair play and friendly consideration. Therefore, I hope the
_____ Tailors will not mind my saying that if they had taken my
measure before writing their letter, their opinion of me would have
been a better fit.[9]

The following year Robinson again directed a choice range of
productions, including another play by Shaw and works by
Goldsmith, Dunsany, Murray, and Ervine. That year also Robinson further exhibited his versatility as a writer when he brought
out a slender volume of his short stories under the title *Eight
Short Stories*. Written between 1912 and 1919, these are, in the
main, either psychological vignettes or brief tales dealing with
the macabre, the preternatural, and the mystic forces shaping
people's lives. "A Pair of Muddy Shoes"—the best of these "Tales
of the Uneasy," as Robinson described them—was reprinted in a
special publisher's selection, *Georgian Stories for 1922*. Another
of Robinson's stories somewhat in the same vein, "Quest," which
Marianne Moore published in *The Dial*, received the honor of also
being included in Edward J. O'Brien's anthology, *The Best British Short Stories of 1927*.

Not unexpectedly, Robinson's psychological sketches in *Eight
Short Stories* suggest that he wrote them as if he had the stage in
mind. He selects some noticeably dramatic episodes and then
depends upon dialogue to advance his stories. The most appealing of these pieces, "The Chalice," which sketches a sympathetic
portrait of a minister of the Church of Ireland, Robinson derived from memories of his father and from an ornate chalice that
his father had treasured.

The Abbey to which Robinson came back no longer had the

prosperous air of the Abbey that he left in 1914. The theatre was facing lean days; audiences were dropping off considerably; repertory tours in England, always a sure source of revenue, had been made impossible by World War I; and the leading actors were compelled to depart from Ireland for other shores, leaving behind them a mere handful of young players to serve as the core of any future reorganization. For the sake of the remaining players the theatre struggled gallantly on amid the deep unrest evoked by one of the most stormy phases of Irish history.

Between 1920 and 1921 the Anglo-Irish War reached its height. The "Black and Tans" raged up and down the countryside, kidnapping, looting, burning, and killing in reprisal for their losses. Strict curfew was enforced and rebel Irishmen chased by the "Tans" hid wherever they could.

Robinson gained a good deal of publicity for the Abbey in the English and Irish press when, on February 24, 1921, he produced Terence MacSwiney's *The Revolutionist,* which had been published several years earlier. MacSwiney, the Mayor of Cork, had died four months previously after drawing world attention to the cause of Irish freedom by his long hunger strike in England. Robinson felt that, since the play set forth the ideals for which MacSwiney died, it would be quite relevant to the times. The British forces, though, never raided the Abbey for this act of defiance; indeed, they seemed to have ignored it all during those troubled years.

Robinson later remembered proudly how the Abbey managed to exist during those crucially onerous times: "To my mind those years (not really because I was so closely associated with them) were as gallant as any in the theatre's history, as gallant as the earliest years of the struggle. In the Anglo-Irish war we soon had a curfew which moved slowly back from midnight to eight thirty, but workers in the city preferred to hurry home at five and be safe from bombs and ambushes." [10]

Some of the apprehensions of the Abbey directors were lessened in 1921 when once again English friends, including Galsworthy and Drinkwater, came to the assistance of the directors. J. B. Fagan, the London producer, arranged a series of rather successful lectures at one of which Shaw read part of his unpublished *Back to Methuselah.* In advertising the lectures, Robinson summarized the Abbey's problems, revealing the fact that the

theatre was in debt for nearly £1000. As his contribution to the
Abbey Fund, Robinson, while in London, arranged for special
matinees of *The Whiteheaded Boy,* then in the middle of a very
successful run at the Ambassador Theatre.

Prospects brightened for the Abbey when the Anglo-Irish
Treaty at the end of 1921 gave Ireland its long-sought independence. But this afforded only a short respite to the embattled little
theatre; for within six months, Ireland was faced with a civil
war, a war as bad if not worse than its grim predecessor. The nation was shocked when the Republican Party under De Valera engaged in a bloody struggle with the Free State Government.

Robinson was greatly upset because he thought the new state
represented an excellent opportunity for Ireland. Besides, he was
impressed by the imagination of such figures in the government
as Collins, O'Higgins, and Bryan Cooper, the Anglo-Irish landlord, whose biography he wrote in 1931. With leaders of their
caliber, Ireland, Robinson believed, could become another Second Empire. So when A. E. pessimistically urged that some dramatist should rewrite Yeats's *Kathleen ni Houlihan* and depict the
beautiful heroine at the end as a reviling old hag, Robinson felt
like following A.E.'s suggestion and going into exile on the day
before the play's production.[11]

The affairs of the Abbey were disrupted just as badly as heretofore; it faced bankruptcy. Yeats saw no hope for its continuance.
More than this, the theatre, as Robinson revealed, was also un-
wittingly drawn into the current whirlpool of political events
as one party countermanded the orders of the other:

I remember vividly the St. Patrick's day of 1923. Two days before I had
received an official communication from the Republicans stating that all
places of amusement must be closed as the country was in a state of
emergency. If we did not obey—well, we must take the consequences.
Two days later the Free State Government sent a somewhat similar pro-
nouncement but it said we were to keep the theatre open. . . . But
I reflected that we had never suffered dictation from Dublin Castle or
mob, it seemed to me we could not now surrender our independence.[12]

Strangely yet happily these adversities only seemed to gener-
ate fresh life in the Abbey's wearied body. For, within two years
after Robinson's return, he could observe that creatively the Abbey's fortunes were taking a turn for the better. Brinsley Mac-

Namara extended his talent as a writer of novels and submitted a series of meritorious plays to the Abbey. Quickly following him came the Ulster dramatist, George Shiels, whose comedies won him a wide popular following. Further, Robinson, himself, in 1922 contributed two novel comedies, one being glowingly received. Then in 1923, the brilliant work of Sean O'Casey very auspiciously began to give the Irish theatre its greatest vigor since the days of Synge. The work of these writers kept the Abbey alive and, over the years, even made a profit for it.

In the middle of 1921 Lady Gregory and Robinson received O'Casey's first manuscripts and had to puzzle through them, since they were written in difficult long hand. "After reading ten pages," said Robinson, "one felt inclined to throw the manuscript aside and reach for a rejection slip, but then suddenly one would come on a character or a scene startling in its truth and originality, a flash of undoubted genius. . . . We never troubled Yeats with hopeless plays, but Mr. O'Casey's plays did hold out hope." [13]

At the outset O'Casey was appreciative of the helpful comments and advice of the directors on his early scripts. In a long chat with Holloway, O'Casey said that he could "never forget the encouragement given by Yeats, Lady Gregory, and Robinson. What would he be only for the Abbey and the playing of the fine company." [14] But some years afterwards, O'Casey bitterly quarreled with Robinson and Yeats over their criticism of *The Silver Tassie* when they rejected it. Still, Robinson did comment that he was pleased to see O'Casey searching for a new style and for different settings.

Before this row, O'Casey and Robinson were not on the most intimate terms. Robinson, though, made overtures to O'Casey on several occasions; he invited him, for instance, to the monthly dinners of the 13 Club to talk about plays for the Drama League and to see a production of Yeats's *The Hawk's Well* in the drawing room of Yeats's home in Merrion Square.

Relations between them were also strained when Robinson mislaid for almost a year O'Casey's only manuscript for *The Plough and the Stars*. While Robinson was rehearsing *The Plough* in 1926, O'Casey thought that Robinson, nervous at the protests of the actors over the lines, "was inclined to be irritable" and "abrupt when he ventured to make suggestions." [15]

On O'Casey's last visit to Ireland in 1936, Robinson invited him to his home in Dalkey. "I would have refused," writes O'Casey, "but Mrs. O'Casey persuaded me to accept the invitation, so we went to see the gulls over Sorrento, and indeed, Mr. Robinson and his wife were charming hosts. When I came back to England, I got but one letter from him which asked me to let him put my name forward for membership of the Irish Academy of Letters; a request I refused." [16]

The Abbey directorate honored Robinson in 1923 by appointing him a fellow director on the Board, a position that he held for the remainder of his life. He also continued as a producer until the arrival of Hugh Hunt in 1935; after that, Robinson rarely directed for the Abbey. Several years prior to Hunt's appointment, Robinson asked Sir Tyrone Guthrie to come as producer, but he was not free at the time. [17]

The financial problems of the Abbey had worsened to such an extent by the end of 1923 that Yeats and Lady Gregory thought of giving the theatre over to the government. Early in the next year, Robinson, then rehearsing his little comedy *Never the Time and the Place,* agreed to act as the theatre's spokesman and to explain matters to Senator Desmond Fitzgerald, whose play he had directed a few years previously. Ultimately, at the suggestion of Minister of Finance Ernest Blythe, now managing director of the Abbey, the government decided in 1924 to recognize the Abbey as the official National Theatre of Ireland and to grant it an annual subsidy. So the Abbey achieved the distinction of being the first government-supported theatre in the English-speaking world.

Robinson added further to his theatrical activities in January of the same year when he replaced St. John Ervine as writer of the weekly "At the Play" column for *The Observer* in London. His newspaper assignment, which lasted until August, 1925, allowed him to retain his residence in Dublin. Meanwhile, to gather the requisite contents for his weekly critical reviews, he made frequent visits to London to see as many plays as he could.

As a drama critic, he made known that he went to the theatre with the hope that he might "be compelled to suffer pain." [18] Mirroring his Dublin interests, he began his reviewing with a series

of three columns on the Abbey Theatre and then went on in
other articles to favor a National Theatre for England and to encourage the Scottish National Theatre. Nor did Robinson forget
about his ties with the Dublin Drama League, for he not only
commended the work of the British Drama League but also devoted many of his columns to discussions of the plays of Ibsen,
Strindberg, Pirandello, O'Neill, Tolstoi, Shaw, and Benavente
and other Spanish dramatists.

The summer of 1924 marked another very stormy session in
Robinson's life. Offended religious sensibilities, and not politics,
were the cause this time. The commotion arose from a tale of his
based upon a delicate subject matter: the rape of a young girl
who imagines herself to be a Madonna. Robinson had written
the story in New York in 1911, during the first tour of the Abbey
Company. He sent it to an English weekly which returned it for
fear it would be offensive. He afterwards submitted it to an
American magazine which, he said, "published it, and there
was no word of reproach from its readers. Then some friends
started a little weekly paper called *Tomorrow* and asked me to
contribute to the first number. I was too busy to write anything
specially for it, but I thought of this little story. The first number—only two numbers appeared—had brilliant contributions
but all were on rather audacious lines." [19]

On account of this story, Father Finlay, S. J.—Robinson's fellow
member on the Central Advisory Committee of the Carnegie
Trust—resigned in protest. The provost of Trinity College also
supported Father Finlay's action. In such wise Robinson was
brought head on into a ticklish situation. Lady Gregory, active
on the same committee, was able to record what went on behind the scenes in Robinson's personal drama:

Yeats says that Stuarts' little paper "Tomorrow" caused a great sensa-
tion. It was rumoured that the Government intended to suppress it. He
went to see Blythe who said Cosgrave had recently thought of doing so,
not because of anything said in it, but because some man, a German,
who is anti-Church, had written saying Lennox Robinson's idea of the
foundations of Christianity in his story is probably the right one, and
Cosgrave is afraid Robinson is a disciple of his and is trying to pervert
the nation. However, the next number is to contain an article in favour
of giving over the cathedrals now in Protestant hands to the Catholics,
and that will puzzle them.[20]

The Carnegie Committee demanded Robinson's resignation which he refused to give. Then, after much argument, he was dismissed. Robinson deeply regretted the aftermath of this affair; it was, he confessed, "inexpressibly painful for me. It alienated many of my Catholic friends." [21]

III *Three Comedies*

Six years intervened between *The Whiteheaded Boy* and the playwright's next comedies, *The Round Table* and *Crabbed Youth and Age,* both staged in 1922. These were followed two years later by a brief satirical play, *Never the Time and the Place.* That he was able to write at all during those years is a tribute to his zealous energy. As his busy daily schedule indicates, his dedicated service to the Abbey and his office work gave him slight opportunity or scope for much else: "I had little other life outside the Abbey and the Carnegie Trust office. . . . I used to get to the office by ten, and having got a day's work started was at the Theatre shortly after eleven for rehearsal till lunch time. Then back to the office till five, at the theatre again for rehearsals at five-thirty and most evenings attended the performance, and home just at midnight. It sounds a long day and it was a long day, but somehow, late at night and on Sundays, I managed to write two plays: *The Round Table* and *Crabbed Youth and Age.*" [22]

The 1920's were a curious time for dramatists in Ireland. The expressionistic theatre was very much the vogue on the Continent; and if Irish playwrights did not care to imitate this new dramatic technique in their quest for novel literary styles, quite often they found themselves taking refuge in such plays as those written by Noel Coward. This state of flux can also be observed in Robinson's contributions to the theatre during the 1920's and the 1930's. While diligently serving the Abbey, he was able also to take important strides towards fulfilling his hopes of introducing fresh ideas into the Irish theatre to rejuvenate the solidly established Abbey play tradition.

In a lecture at the Abbey entitled "Drama in Dublin," which led to the establishing of the Peacock Theatre in November, 1925, as an experimental adjunct to the Abbey, Robinson had protested against the limitations of the parent theatre; it was entangled in its own success. To remedy this flaw, he prescribed two or three companies to rehearse different classes of productions, without which the theatre could never fully satisfy a critical public. But unfortunately his attempts to give variety to his dramatic interests were to wean him away from what he seems to write best: satirical comedies of Irish life.

If one excepts Lord Dunsany, in whose consciousness Ireland seems to play little part, one may regard the playwright's next creation in his mellow mood, *The Round Table*, as a departure by an Irish dramatist having an Irish audience in mind. This play, which had nothing especially Irish about it, points the way for Robinson's later flights into newer and more cosmopolitan literary regions.

In the first version of the play, which received its opening performance at the Abbey on January 31, 1922, the playwright dramatizes what he called a "comic-tragedy." From his introductory stage directions, some of his earliest flutterings out of Ireland for his material are noticeable: "There are two towns mentioned in this play—Cork and Gloucester. Their significance is that Cork should be a town not very far distant from the town in which the play is performed, while Gloucester should be a considerable distance away. Thus, if the play were produced in London, 'Cork' might be Reading and 'Gloucester' Aberdeen."

The title, *The Round Table*, is a symbolic one. To Daisy Drennan, the central and most normal character in the play, her "round table" represents all that is monotonous and inhibiting in her life. In a fashion, Robinson, through the deep-rooted promptings of Daisy's spirit, comes back to a subject he had formerly used, the conflict of the dreamer with reality; only here the dreams of Daisy are subconscious and not in the foreground. They inspire her to escape the dreary demands of her home life and go off in search of an ideal world where her imagination will be enchanted by exotic beauty, where she will not suffer the defeat and disillusionment that the playwright's previous visionary characters have suffered.

The comedy rises from the individualistic antics of the members of the Drennan family, who luckily have the intelligent and very competent Daisy to guide them. They have come to rely so much on her directions that they find it impossible to get along without her. Their widowed mother, whose talk—like Mrs. Nickleby's—runs on in an aimless and endless flow of speech, has brought up her children in a most haphazard fashion. The family includes a stamp-collecting younger sister, a yogi-conscious younger brother, the most self-centered of eldest brothers, and Mrs. Williams–Williams or "Billy-Billy," the most dismal of poor relations. This unique ménage depends so much on Daisy for comfort and order that the family is aghast when she announces her proposed marriage to Chris Pegum, a rather unimaginative but sound young man. Of course, they all love her for herself, and nothing is good enough for Daisy. But it is preposterous of her to think of deserting them. This part of the play affords Robinson a chance to show some of his best talents in his sly, ironic thrusts. Such touches would suggest that he intended to develop the play as pure comedy.

Daisy, confronted with the discontented Drennans, has to arrange some program that will allow her to marry. She draws upon all her efficiency and her firmness of will. She satisfies her mother by persuading her to live with Chris's mother. In the eldest boy, she ultimately stimulates enough regard for marriage to impel him to culminate happily his own four-year engagement. Finally, she encourages a shy, stamp-collecting suitor to propose to her stamp-collecting sister. Her problems apparently are well solved, but the burdens she has been facing affect her nerves. Her tired brain imagines that at the window it sees a face which she thinks is the image of her own. Then the hard-driving Daisy faints. In delaying Daisy's motivation for her later strange actions until the end of the first act, Robinson considerably weakens her value as a character and clothes his work with an air of implausibility.

During the second act, the face reappears at the window. Going to the window, Daisy notices a young woman of her own age whose air of independence fascinates her. Her curiosity is aroused and she probes into the woman's background. After questioning her, Daisy realizes that the romantic independence of the strange young woman, who has left her husband and child to wander the earth, offers her glimpses of her own innerself. Like an enchantress, the woman conjures up for Daisy an alluring picture of exotic places:

The Woman   No place is as good as any other place. No two souls are alike and no two places are alike.—One day something—I don't know what—seemed to happen to me—something snapped. I said to myself: I'm here in an amazing world. I didn't ask to come here but here I am. Soon I will die. I'll go out of this world into something—no one knows what—or into nothing. . . . I can see this strange beautiful terrible world, touch it, listen to it. . . . If I had stayed in Gloucester, a night like this might have made me miserable—but not now. Do you know what I do—I shut my eyes and forget the rain and the cold and think of the wonderful places I've seen.

Daisy (Yearningly) Paris, I suppose? And, perhaps, Rome?

The Woman There are better places than Paris. Little strange towns, Algeciras, for instance, very early on a summer morning with the air black with screaming swallows against a very blue sky. A white town in North Africa all sunlight and dark shadows, and a very grey little town in Austria. I've forgotten its name—cloistered on a rocky hill in a long valley all dark with pine woods and great hills in the distance just tipped with snow. . . .

Daisy I've lived in this place all my life and I'm not bored.

The Woman Aren't you? I get terribly bored. . . . And I am free.

Daisy Free? Oh, yes, mustn't that be wonderful! But you can get that without going away, without kicking over the traces as you have done. . . . Oh, you know there's a round polished table in my bedroom, it stands in the window. Every day I dust it, in summer, twice a day—three times—and every day the dust comes floating through the window and settles on it. I can lie in bed and watch the dust drifting in. Lately I've felt I could smash that table with a hatchet and make kindling of it. I'll sell it, I'll be free of it, I'll be free of the whole thing at last. . . .

In the final act, which descends to farce, Robinson's flair for introducing whimsy at odd moments is noticeable. He unexpectedly inserts a drunken passenger who wanders aimlessly in and out of the station waiting room, where all the celebrating Drennans assemble to send off the newlyweds. While at the station with the others, Daisy has another quick vision of the strange woman, her true self. There and then she puts an end to her own delayed marriage plans with the now thoroughly surprised Chris and obeys the secret yearnings of her heart:

Daisy I give and bequeath you my round table.

The Mellowed Mood

Chris   What table?

Daisy   All the silly things that we do again and again, this stupid going round and round the mulberry bush, this dance that leads to nowhere. Goodbye! . . .

Chris   You're either a fool or mad.

Daisy   Perhaps both, but at any rate happier than I've ever been in my life. Always I've been afraid of tomorrow, of what might happen; now I feel I should like to kiss life on the lips whatever it brings me. . . . I'm like a little child in a suburban garden climbing to the top of the wall to see the world beyond and finding only another garden exactly like the one I've climbed out of, then—then at least there is one sure way out.

Chris   Back to me.

Daisy   No, Chris, not back to you. Just—out. . . . I'm longing to be off.

(She turns to the doorway and speaks mock dramatically):
Look in my face;—my name is "Might-have-been" I'm also called "No more, Too Late, Farewell."

Rather like a Barrie heroine, Daisy departs, leaving behind her an astonished, helpless Chris and a bewildered family, who now cluster around him instead for support and guidance. Chris has misgivings about his new role, but he decides to stand by the family; perhaps the future will untie his fetters: "Some day the tap may come at my window."

This wish of Chris anticipated Robinson's revisions in the new version first staged at the Playhouse Theatre, Liverpool, on March 16, 1927. He made the changes at Yeats's encouragement, for the poet thought that the symbolism of the first version was not effective enough, that it failed to create the proper atmosphere for Daisy's mood. As a result of the alterations, Robinson was obliged to change the category of the play from comic-tragedy to comedy. The chief reason for this difference lies in the ending, which would satisfy Dante's requirements for comedy: it closes on a note of happiness, delight, and charm when Chris, too, decides to follow Daisy in her quest for a land of dreams.

The playwright also introduces a new symbol, ringing bells, to take the place of the former one of the "strange woman."

Whenever Daisy hears them ringing, an inner voice tempts her to travel to exotic places. The substitute proves to be an unsatisfactory one; and the original play, even though it has the tendency to go off on unresolved tangents, remains the better of the two.

The subsequent London production of *The Round Table* was not well attended, provoking James Agate when reviewing the play to berate West-End audiences: "All shame to the playgoers. Here is a technically imperfect play which is many miles, streets, oceans or whatever unit of comparison you prefer—better than 99 per cent of West-End successes." [23]

On November 14, 1922, Robinson brought out his second comedy for that year at the Abbey. Entitled *Crabbed Youth and Age*, it was a carefully knit one-act comedy of manners, one of the few of its kind in the Abbey repertoire. He dedicated it to Sara Purser, a leading artistic personality and the wittiest woman in Dublin at that time. Since the central character was believed to be based on her life, the play won quite a favorable response.

Robinson again departs from the customary "Abbey" play in making this excursion into satire on modern manners. The story is slight, but it is very competently developed, step by step, every part in order. Through an aptly balanced series of contrasts between the poised, experienced mother and her boorish children, Robinson tells his audience that the wisdom and experience a woman gains over the years can charm and attract men far better than the brusqueness of youth.

Robinson's information concerning the construction of his finished work gives one some idea of the pains he took at his craft: "*Crabbed Youth and Age* took me nearly six months of pretty constant work, writing version after version, fore-shortening and further fore-shortening, making it in the end the seemingly careless easy thing I hope it is." [24] Further confirming how earnestly Robinson took his writing are the observations of his closest friend, Norris Davidson, program director of Radio Eireann: "I had many opportunities of seeing him at work. He wrote very seriously almost like someone doing a 9 to 5 job. He wrote direct to the typewriter and never on his knees in odd corners. He made innumerable corrections and then retyped, still making changes, before sending the final version to his typist." [25]

The heroine in *Crabbed Youth and Age*, which Robinson originally called *The Revolt of the Swans*,[26] is Mrs. Swan, a pleasant, middle-aged widow, who has three marriageable daughters. In spite of their youth and education, they are unable to compete with the winning personality of their mother. After many years of experience in dealing with people, she knows most of the subtle feminine ways to attract men. Her daughters, though, are not so gifted; and, because of their brusque manners, they are unable to hold the interest of three young men callers. She, on the other hand, through her personable manners becomes the object of the visitors' attentive admiration, much to her daughters' disgust. In the end she is compelled to come to her daughters' assistance and tell them the secrets that make men find her charming.

So much did this comedy of manners appeal to Yeats that he prefaced his collection of *Essays* in 1924 with a dedication to Robinson: "I have seen your admirable little play . . . and would greet the future. My friends and I loved symbols, popular beliefs and old scraps of verse that made Ireland romantic to herself, but the new Ireland, overwhelmed by responsibility begins to long for psychological truth. You have been set free from your work at the Abbey theatre . . . that you may create another satirical masterpiece."

The dramatist rounded out this stage of his writing career with the brief farce *Never the Time and the Place*. In this very slight offering, first acted at the Abbey on February 19, 1924, the previously noted interest of the playwright in the occult is given a humorous slant through his satire on fortunetelling. The central idea of this uninspired skit lies in the quotation from Browning: "Never the Time and the Place/ And the loved one all together!"

Mrs. Mooney, a middle-aged woman, in her overcrowded room somewhere in the heart of Dublin, earns her living telling fortunes by reading cards and peering into a crystal ball. A shrewd opportunist, she works on the gullibility of her clients; and, although legally she is not entitled to collect fees for her prophecies, she has a policeman among her customers. Ostensibly the money she is given goes to aid missionaries in China. Two of her female clients anxiously seek matrimonial guidance from her, hence the humor in the sketch centers around Mrs. Mooney playing off each woman against the naïve policeman. But in the confusion of errors made by the characters, no one is satisfied.

Ironically, the play ends with Mrs. Mooney as the real winner: "Dear, dear. (She goes to the money box, opens the bottom of it and shakes out the money.) Five shillings, two half-crowns, another five shillings, fifteen shillings altogether. The creatures never knowing their luck when they meet it. Well, it all helps to keep the pot boiling. China—I mean (she pockets the money.)"

Robinson's dramas in the eight years from 1916 to 1924, including also the romantic political play, *The Lost Leader*, evidence a marked ripening of his creative powers. His awareness of the inner promptings of the heart of man is keener, his knowledge of the literary fabric at hand for his fashioning is surer, his sense of craftsmanship developed from a sound practical grounding in the arts and skills of the theatre is more disciplined. In the security of these gradually cultivated powers, he exhibits an optimistic outlook that is not mawkish. Outstanding among the plays of this period are *The Whiteheaded Boy* and *Crabbed Youth and Age;* they show characteristics not seen before: not only controlled exuberance of spirit but also a quiet gaiety of heart.

CHAPTER 5

The Search for Wider Horizons

ROBINSON'S desires to inject fresh blood into the Irish theatre, to vary the substance of his plays and to interpret it differently, had long been prompting him. As early as 1913 his cosmopolitan interests, as already noted, had received their first concrete but somewhat brief expression in his productions of Continental plays at the Abbey. An additional attempt to give rein to these urges aborted a year later when Robinson, at Yeats's prompting, had tried to write a psychological drama concerning marital jealousies. Since there was little hope of the Abbey's putting on his embryo play, owing to its unusual subject matter, he had decided to put it aside.

Now, however, in this period of Robinson's work extending chiefly from 1925 to 1934 he makes a concentrated effort to fulfill his artistic hopes and needs. No longer is he contented with the parochial limitations imposed by the characteristic "Abbey" play, even though he had achieved considerable popular success in a comedy of this genre. Rather, he sees fit to wander beyond the Irish scene for his ideas and inspiration and to break completely from the molds he had helped shape in the Irish theatre up to this time.

Several years before Robinson began these pioneering endeavors, the Irish Civil War had broken out, greatly affecting not only the playwright and Irish writers generally, but also the people of Ireland as a whole. Already in the wake of the partial satisfaction of the hunger for freedom achieved through the Anglo-Irish Treaty, a certain deflation of principles had set in; hence the raw wounds of the nation's body left festering in the struggle of centuries did not get much chance to heal. But the recuperative process completely ceased when the Civil War erupted. Brother fought brother, and family hated family. The resultant spirit of lawlessness only added to the still open sores of the country. On this account Ireland, which had given itself to high hopes and stirring thoughts, found itself now skeptical, discouraged, and disillusioned. For the Irish world this internecine strife brought about a decisive shattering of the early romantic ideals of the founders of the Irish literary revival. The artists' past expectations remained but to mock their seeming gullibility; their defeated and disrupted ideals sharply contrasted with the increasingly vital activities of statesmen, politicians, and businessmen.

During these years of sad unrest, Robinson projects an adventurous course for himself. It reaches a turning point in the significant experimental play *Church Street,* in which the playwright examines himself and his aims, and confesses publicly his failure to find what he was seeking outside Ireland. The dramatist dons a cosmopolitan garb and shows a willingness to experiment, to avoid hackneyed subjects, and to place the drama of the outside world on Ireland's doorstep. Yet this is only an exotic mask serving to hide the playwright's puzzled inner self. Deep in Robinson's subconscious there seems to exist a nagging feeling of uncertainty as he leaves behind the known for the unknown and haltingly gropes his way along strange creative paths. More than this, all the while, he is hampered and depressed by the doubt of ever achieving a satisfactory ending to his search.

I *Activities With the Dublin Drama League*

Much of the internationalism of Robinson could be traced to the tastes of the founders of the Irish literary movement. After immersing themselves in the subtleties of Continental civilization, Yeats and Martyn had already brought back with them to Ireland a refreshing European point of view and had applied it to the spirit of Irish nationalism. Thus they hoped that they might prevent Irish patriotism from being too inbred and too narrow. Robinson, too, desirous of fruitfully experiencing the refinements of European culture, traveled frequently and extensively on the Continent, accompanying Yeats on several occasions.

Robinson's aspirations to extend the horizons of the Irish theatre led him in the autumn of 1918 to promote the Dublin Drama League, similar to the London Stage Society or to the Drama League in the United States. Encouraging and supporting him were Yeats, James Stephens, and Ernest Boyd. His letter to James

Stephens, from Limerick, dated September 27, 1918, set forth his objectives and plans:

> For a considerable time I have been thinking and talking about the desirability of establishing in Dublin some organization for the purpose of securing productions of plays which we otherwise would have no chance of seeing. Mr. Yeats, I found was thinking the same thing and we have now discussed the matter together and roughly mapped out a scheme. Our activities would start with a meeting of the Arts Club to which people likely to be interested would be invited and I want to know whether you would consent to your name being one of the four names attached to the enclosed letter of invitation. The letter cannot give many details and you will probably like to know more about it before committing yourself. Yeats is in Dublin—at the Stephens' Green Club—and will tell you all about it. At any rate I beg of you not to send me a hasty refusal before you have seen him.[1]

The four promoters then sent out a circular letter calling for a meeting at the United Arts Club in Dublin on October 8 and explaining the purpose of the venture. They pointed out that growing dissatisfaction prevailed in Dublin about the kind of plays presented there. The repertoire of the touring companies tended to be increasingly limited in range, since they put on only those works which appealed to large audiences. This being so, there were fewer opportunities for Irish theatregoers to appreciate less popular but more artistic dramas. The minority, nonetheless, each winter could secure the production of five or six plays which in the ordinary course of events would not be seen in Dublin. Such a goal, the organizers explained, could be obtained in three ways: "Companies on tour with a play the League wished to see might be attracted to Dublin by a guarantee; existing companies in Dublin might be asked by the League to produce an 'unpopular' play in return for the League's support; the League might commission a producer in Dublin to present a particular play for them." [2]

When choosing dramas suitable for the needs of the League, Robinson depended principally upon the works of modern European and American dramatists. His eclectic selections merited the praise of Denis Johnston, whose dynamic expressionistic plays the League inspired: "Lennox and the Drama League really did remarkable work in the twenties and early thirties in introducing to Dublin all the *avant garde* plays of the time. He did not understand or like expressionism. He left this to Arthur Shields and later to me. But he, and the older generation that he represented, taught us and showed us Strindberg, Pirandello, Benavente, Schnitzler, people whose plays we would never have seen—and maybe not even have read, if it hadn't been for the Drama League." [3]

Shortly after Robinson moved from his cottage on Sir Horace Plunkett's estate sometime in 1925 to a house called "Sorrento" in Dalkey, County Dublin, he expanded his Drama League activities. There, amid the decorative surroundings of his attractive home, he produced and sometimes acted in Greek plays, among them *The Cyclops* and *Iphigenia in Tauris* of Euripides. His stage was a natural one for outdoor performances. The front of his house overlooked delightful Killiney Bay, and at the back were sloping, terraced gardens. To these performances came Lady Gregory, Yeats, Walter Starkie, A. E., Rutherford Mayne, Denis Johnston, actors and actresses from Dublin theatres, and such visiting friends as Shaw, James Bridie, and Lord Dunsany. For those guests who liked a variation from the serious discussions following each production, Robinson's invitations always included "swimming afterwards."

As a prelude to the League's activities both Yeats and Robinson weighed the merits and demerits of the new venture at a public discussion held at the Abbey. Yeats, restating Synge's arguments, pointed out that time and the retention of an absorbing interest in Ireland would eventually assist playwrights to give better plays to the Abbey. With this reasoning Robinson did not agree; and in an admirable synthesis of his own views, he went on to defend the League:

> One gets one's most vivid inspiration by being brought into contact with a passionate situation created by an artist. . . . Here in Ireland we are isolated, cut off from the thought of the world, except the English world, and from England we get little, in drama, except fourthrate. I ask you, for the young writer's sake, to open up the door and let us out of our prison. Seeing foreign plays will not divorce our minds from Ireland. . . . but being brought into touch with other minds who have different values for life, suddenly we shall discover the rich material that lies to our hand in Ireland. 'Will you seek afar off? You surely come back at last. In things best known to you finding the best,' Whitman says. But to make that discovery we must travel.[4]

From the beginning then, Robinson closely associated himself with the League, acting first of all as its secretary. Ultimately in 1929 he assumed the presidency that Yeats vacated. Besides these administrative responsibilities, he also directed a large number of the League's performances, and he successfully acted in several of them under the stage name of "Paul Ruttledge," the hero of Yeats's mystical *Where There is Nothing*.

Holloway, a sound judge of acting, greatly admired Robinson's playing. He, for instance, lauded him as the king in Pirandello's *Henry IV*, for "a great personal success. His height, thinness and sharpness of profile all tended to make a memorable stage picture." [5] Subsequently, Holloway came away well pleased after watching Robinson acting as Edgar, with Barry Fitzgerald as Curt, in Strindberg's *Dance of Death*: "He gave a surprisingly interesting study of the self willed, suspicious disagreeable egoist and weaved a web of uncanniness about the ever-complaining wreck of a man." [6] So affecting, in fact, was this play that it led to a vogue for Strindberg among the Dublin literati.

The distinction of Robinson's performances surprised his audiences who up to now had thought of him chiefly as a playwright or as a play director. So, when the critics took too lightly the planning and care he expended to achieve his effect of apparently effortless acting, he was moved to protest: "If I played a Strindberg madman—in *The Father*—they simply said, 'Well, of course, Lennox Robinson is mad; there's no acting in that.' And if I sweated very hard over Lewis Dodd—'But he's exactly that type, artistic and all that sort of thing. He's very good, of course, but there's no acting there. He is "Lewis Dodd." ' But when I acted a God no one said that in real life I was divine." [7]

II *Cosmopolitanism and Pessimism*

After such experiences of the revolutionary forces in the international theatre, it was only natural that Robinson's thought and art should reflect his engrossment in them. As an eager student of European and American drama, he was especially attracted to the plays of Pirandello, Strindberg, O'Neill, and Rice, but more especially to those of the Spanish playwrights: Benavente, Sierra, and the Quintero brothers. The similarity of certain aspects of life in Spain and Ireland might help to explain the greater appeal of the Spanish writers for Robinson.[8]

With his *Portrait, a Play in Two Sittings*, first acted under his direction at the Abbey on March 31, 1925, Robinson prompted a trend in Ireland towards the writing of psychological dramas about the world of the prospering middle class. With *Portrait*, too, he initiated a series of his own plays, which image the effects of the Civil War on his spirit; for running through them is a strong undercurrent of pessimism, "his tendency to gloom." [9] One can notice in them that, when the playwright tries to penetrate into the deeper recesses of the minds of his characters, he selects, not heroes of the same caliber as James Nugent, but outwardly small people who do not bother to think of the existence of such a thing as tragedy. But, when tragedy does strike, it forces them into an ironic situation over which they apparently have no control.

Part of the fresh countenance of *Portrait* Robinson owes to the shaping hands of Benavente, several of whose plays the Drama League produced during the years 1924 and 1925. The uniqueness of Benavente's dramatic technique stems from his assumption that the best of any artist's genius is not what is explained in his works but what escapes from them. Benavente, therefore, does not bother to give lengthy stage directions; the characters express all that is necessary for the audience to know. Also, instead of the conventional plots of the regular realistic drama, he unfolds a series of correlated little incidents rather similar to the mode of the cinema.

One Benaventian mannerism that Robinson uses in *Portrait* is the lack of stage directions; they are down to the barest minimum. Robinson's form also is Benaventian, for he projects a study of jealousy and inconstancy through the contrasts established in what he calls "two sittings." He sets in opposition the forceful people against the meek and the old against the young. Then to add greater intensity to his dramatic conflict, he contrasts a weak male with a strong woman. For his setting Robinson compares the innocent, simple pleasures of the Barnados, comfortable middle-class parents, with their restless, jazz-conscious children. The parents spend their time recalling old memories and reading Dickens, while the young giddily play the latest jazz recordings and make love.

Maggie, their unmarried daughter, is engaged to an intelligent but unaggressive man. The parents have approved the common-sense characteristics of their prospective son-in-law, Peter; and, with the expectation that Peter will seek for promotion, they look forward to their daughter's marrying soon. Just the same, Peter has one serious failing in the eyes of Maggie. Sympathetic with the assertive traits of her friends, she views his great diffidence with grave misgivings. While she wants the earth for her children, he has no desire to push anyone aside to get ahead in the world. To him life with all its ambitious striving is a distasteful affair, a complex riddle that appears to have no answer. Because Peter, whom she would like to love, does not come up to her model of the vigorous, savage, masterful type she admires, she threatens that she will seek elsewhere for her ideal. Her married sister, Mary, who—like the unknown woman in *The Round Table*—has left her husband and child, suggests that Tom Hughes is the man her sister wants. Mary, too, is imbued with the harshly pragmatic attributes of her sister.

In the "second sitting," the young have assembled for a masquerade dance at Peter's middle-class home. Peter has refused to accept his promotion because it means brushing aside a deserving colleague. While drinking heavily to bolster up his courage before breaking the news to Maggie, he analyzes himself and becomes mockingly self-critical. He cannot discover any satisfaction within himself to give life some meaning, and in his drunken utterances he confesses that life taunts and mocks him. Out of the vagueness of Peter's gropings, however, arises the weakness of the play; it gives an inkling of the playwright's uncertainty about his conception of the significance of Peter's role in the tragedy. Peter tries to explain his problem to his brother:

Peter . . . if only there were any way to see. "I am the Way, the Truth and the Life." Quotations again. But suppose, after all, it happened to be true?

Charlie What?

Peter Christ.

Shortly Peter hears that Maggie is finally giving him up for the more virile Tom. Her refusal wounds him greatly. Nothing else matters to him now but the thought of leaving one lasting final impression. Since he was able to dodge life's problems before, he plans to do it again, this time in a more dramatic fashion. He seizes the gun Tom has brought to the masquerade. When Tom warns him it is loaded, Peter says: "Loaded? I should hope so. Of what use is an impotent God? Even I, now that I have it in my hands feel its terrific power. I—the meek one . . . of course, that's it! Do you remember, Maggie; my saying that the meek shall inherit the earth, and wondering how the devil they could if they are meek? Why, of course, it's true, it's all they can inherit—six feet of it—like this (He shoots himself)."

And so the play concludes on this fantastic, macabre note. To cover up the noise of the shot from Peter's inquiring parents, Maggie, dressed in Spanish costume, dances around the room to the music of the victrola. When the shock finally hits her, she dashes out of the room, leaving the record loudly playing, "Tonight, we'll merry, merry be."

Before Robinson produced his next play, *The White Blackbird*, at the Abbey for the first time seven months later on October 12, the doubtful morality of its ending prevented full approval by all the directors on the Abbey board. One of the conservative members had consulted outside advisers as to whether the suggestion of incest in the last act should not debar the play from the Abbey.[10] All the same, it was passed, lest it might be said that the government was unduly interfering with the liberty of the theatre.[11]

In *The White Blackbird* the playwright returns to the same middle-class milieu he dramatized in *Portrait*. He also reverts to the same uncertain groping about his objectives and purposes already noted in the previous fashioning of the contents of his plays. Presumably he intended to make this drama into a reflection on the selfish and petty qualities and manners existing in some upper middle-class families.

The White Blackbird takes its "Ibsenish" title from the dominant trait of the central figure, William, who is a bird alone that never sings. His mother has taken illegal possession of an estate that his father had willed to him before going forth to a seemingly accidental death in the Swiss Alps. In truth, his nagging, shrewish wife had forced him into suicide.

As the play opens, one learns that William has grown up into a strong-willed but lonely young man, who craves affection and sympathy. His mother has married a Mr. Naynoe, a feckless person, as his name suggests; and with her other children, two daughters and a son, she lives a life of luxury on the falsely acquired property. But William, after a protracted legal squabble about the ownership of the estate, obtains rightful control.

Now it is the turn of the pampered members of the Naynoe family, who never thought it necessary to earn a living, to face facts for a change. William, nevertheless, does not take revenge for their niggardly treatment of him. He sets out, instead, to redeem them from their selfish ways; he offers to finance the eldest daughter's wedding, and he forces his dissipated step-brother, Tinker, to go off to work in a Spanish mine as a preparation for a subsequent job in the family mine at home. Only Bella, the youngest, gives him any satisfying response when he offers to send her to art school to train her innate artistic abilities. Through Bella, Robinson introduces a lightly humorous note into a seriously treated subject. His subtle laughter is attained through the tolerantly amused attitude that he frequently adopts towards his young characters.

In the last act the play moves on to a most inconclusive ending, and the theme of the play is lost in the confusion of events. One is curiously disturbed about what feeling to have for William. Should one like him, or despise him, or smile at him? When the day of the wedding of the eldest daughter arrives, Tinker returns with a woman, ostensibly his wife, but really a prostitute. At the instigation of Tinker, she tries to seduce William; but she fails to dethrone him from his position as the strong man of the family. Even though William is a victor over them in their schemes to oust him, he is a loser in his endeavors to gain friends. He is left a solitary, loveless figure, and only Bella remains to offer him slight consolation. Her winning frankness attracts him, so he suggests he would like to marry her. But this prospect is left dangling, and William at the end is obliged to seek solace in his work as manager of the family mine:

William   Money—I don't need it, but I want to make lots of it. God knows why. And power . . . I couldn't live if life could be explained! Could you, Bella? You understand me, don't you?

Bella   (Sleepily—her head buried in the cushion). Oh, quite, quite, go on.

William   You understand—and that's all I want. I don't mind being alone, I don't mind loneliness. You can laugh at me as much as you

like and call me strong and silent. I am, it's all I can be. And I've got music, and the ghost as mother calls it. It's enough Bella, isn't it? (She doesn't answer) Asleep? So even you don't understand. (He looks out of the window.) One should see the white blackbird now; there is nothing but two sparrows fighting. (on the phone)
Yes, is that Miller? . . . I'll be down at the works in about half an hour.
Yes, I'll be there all day. Right. (He rings off, he looks at Bella sleeping) I expect it's a damned good thing for both of us that I can't marry you.

For the germ idea of his next pessimistic play, Robinson is indebted to the popular proverb, "Give a Dog." Even though one knows the upshot of giving a dog a bad name, one tends to ignore the consequences and to widen its scope with more idle talk, half-truths, and innuendoes until the outcome becomes a tragedy. Robinson also stages the inevitable tragic ending arising from similar circumstances, but he depends on an accidental death to unravel the chief complication of his plot.

Give a Dog, written in 1927 and published in 1928, had trying days ahead before it reached the stage for the first time. The Abbey Board of Directors would not accept it for presentation because of its unpleasant subject matter, making it the first of Robinson's plays they refused. Some of the difficulty arising from the contents of Give a Dog can be deduced from the comments of Lady Gregory to the playwright: "I'm fretting about the play, trying to think it would be all right. . . . I tried to put you out of my head and write one of my usual reports of plays sent in and enclose result. What worries me is that W. B. Y. is evidently in no state to be consulted, and also after all your kindness and help to me in my play I would seem so ungracious but I have tried to unthink my first impression but in vain; it has given me bad nights and I may be getting into senility and should resign." [12]
A few days later she again agonized over the play with Robinson: "You are not more distressed than I am. I have been quite miserable these last days. I hope you have not spoken to anyone about it, rumours would do us all, Abbey and all, harm. It would be wrong to withdraw it on my judgment alone—unfair to you and me, what is needed is an outside opinion. The love of the Abbey is a very terrible thing." [13]
In the end, Give a Dog achieved its premiere on January 20,

1929, at the Strand Theatre, London, where it closed after the second night. It did not come to Dublin until May 12 of the same year; then the Drama League gave a performance of it at the Abbey. A weekly newspaper in the city, as a satire upon the event, hired a sandwich man to parade in front of the Abbey: the sign he carried read "The Wickedness of Lennox Robinson."

In this erratically conceived play, Philip Barrett, a rather clever young architect, thinks that the ultrarespectable segment of society in which he moves is drying up the springs of his creative inspiration. He regards the inhibitions of his narrow circle as sources of frustration that block his freedom as an artist at every turn—so much so that he believes himself to be a burden to the firm of architects for which he works. One thought now fascinates him. Was not the original founder of the firm able to combine brilliance with a dissolute life; perhaps there may be a correlation between the two?

Milly Wheaton, a chorus girl in a visiting theatrical troupe, might have helped him clarify his vagueness if he had known her earlier in his life. Upon assisting her one night as she comes staggering home from the theatre, he enters into a series of events which cause consternation among his smug friends. Little do they realize Milly's innocent reasons for her intoxicated state. Her theatrical colleagues, with the best of intentions, had generously helped her to follow the advice of dissipated Dr. Pobjoy, a disillusioned local doctor, who had prescribed whisky to relieve her pains.

Philip, while driving Milly home in his car, crashes into a lamp post; gossip about him quickly spreads all over town, and soon his once reputable name is held in low esteem. Is he not a seducer of chorus girls and what is more—a man who spends his time composing blasphemous poems and smutty limericks? After being told about the accident, his smug fiancée as well as his snobbish friends and acquaintances shun him.

Meantime, Sidney Prade, his only remaining friend, proposes giving a supper party for Milly to compensate the girl for her misfortune. In a typical "Noel Coward" scene, Milly and another chorus girl join the two men at Philip's apartment, and a sequence of chance happenings forces Milly to stay the night with Philip. Next morning he finds her dead in his bedroom. This catastrophe brings to the surface a hidden side of Philip. He sees himself as a lonely figure groping for a meaning to life, thus Milly's loneliness is like his. He refuses to take the advice of his mother and of his very proper uncle, Major Barrett, to leave for America and reshape his career there. Why not remain, he reasons with himself, and, in the strength of his new inspiration, begin life afresh at home:

Philip   . . . suddenly I've been delivered by a miracle—by God.

Major   By a scandalous tragedy, by a common chorus girl—

Philip   The angel of God . . . she never seemed quite real . . . A Blake drawing . . . a foundling . . . alone . . . a dream. It's a dream that she ever kissed me and died. Why, if that door were to open now and she were to walk in I wouldn't be surprised. Look, it is opening, isn't it? No, that's the mystery, she's dead, she had to die to save me—or perhaps I had to be ruined to save her, she's safe, she's gone on somewhere—and I must go on too. Do you remember, on some Greek vase, "Orestes pursued by the Furies"?

Mrs. Barrett   You're not, I won't have you say such things. God isn't like that, He's pitiful and kind.

Philip   No, pitiless. There's something in me He wants said—done—a beautiful building or two—He tried the soft way, position and money, marriage—no use. I had to be broken. Stripped of everything decent. Alone.

In this passage, the playwright discloses the play's underlying idea: genius must be left free as the air; respectability kills it. But this somewhat vague and muddled mysticism and the confusion arising from the interweaving of the lesser themes in the course of the drama leave *Give a Dog* completely without any unity of form or purpose. Several questions that the author poses remain unanswered in his subsidiary ideas. Can happiness in life be realized, as Milly believes, by taking what comes? Or can it be acquired, as Major Barrett maintains, by being respectable? Or can it be achieved, as Philip thinks, by unfettering genius? But perhaps the playwright's answer really lies in Pobjoy's despairing remark to Philip's housekeeper, Mrs. Enright, before the curtain falls:

Pobjoy   It's all such a cod, isn't it? Life. Little things get us and we don't know where we are. Philip says it's God. Is it?

Mrs. Enright How do I know? She's dead and he's in gaol.

Pobjoy For three days. And ten to one it will make a genius of him. And I suppose I should have been in gaol ten times but it wouldn't have made anything of me. Life? It's all a cod. (He reaches for the whisky)

—Curtain—

All's Over Then?, first produced under Robinson's direction at the Abbey on July 25, 1932, before a packed and enthusiastic house, brings to a close this somber phase of his writing career. To a marked degree this drama displays the appeal that Strindberg had for him both in his choice of subject and in his handling of it. Since Strindberg viewed life as essentially dominated by strife between the sexes, what could be more alluring to him for dramatization than an intense battle of man against woman for domination and power. In this clash, moreover, woman is the evil one, for it is her nature to destroy her mate once she has used him.

Robinson, too, in *All's Over Then?*, mindful of Strindberg's *The Father*, delineates a conflict of a dominant woman striving to manipulate all of her husband's actions. The ensuing struggle affords the playwright the opportunity to attempt a psychological study of female neurosis and frustrated love. Unfortunately, though, Robinson destroys once again the inevitability of his potential tragedy, in as much as he depends on melodrama to solve his dramatic problems; only his expert technique saves his work from complete unreality.

The Swinnertons are an intelligent, cultivated family. Henry, a writer of dull biographies, is a pleasant but weak-willed man. Eleanore, his very neurotic wife, feels very conscious of the age difference between herself and her husband. Morbidly sensitive about her age, she is fearful that her husband, younger by eleven years, will cease loving her. Her dread is intensified by the return of their daughter, Maggie, a capable young novelist. Both women adore this weakling male, but the daughter becomes more and more attached to the father. To offset this growing affection, Eleanore drops hints to her gullible husband that he is showing the effects of his age, that he needs rest and a change for his health. Perhaps he would benefit from a trip to Italy, where he can do leisurely research for another biography.

Eleanore also showers her attentions on her daughter; but Maggie becomes suspicious of her mother, especially when she urges her to marry a suitor with little appeal to her artistic nature. Besides, she has not forgotten the fact that her mother purposefully kept her away from home for over eleven years. Maggie soon unmasks her mother's camouflaged affection and bares the jealousy that torments her. She is so emotionally upset at her mother's revelations that she has to be escorted to the bedroom for rest. In the implausible, melodramatic scene that follows, Maggie, afraid that she will not sleep, asks her mother for a sleeping potion. Then, assuming her daughter to be asleep, Eleanore shuts the windows and turns on the gas jet in the bedroom. So the act ends with the mother, as she locks the door behind her, "gazing in hate" at Maggie.

This melodramatic suspense reaches its peak in the third act in which one learns that Maggie was not fully asleep after all and had retained enough presence of mind to break the window pane and to save herself in time. Eleanore, now completely frustrated, makes a full confession to her thoroughly shocked and disgusted husband. In her neurotic self-pity she excoriates him for never fully knowing her inner needs:

What a fool I've been, I've damned my soul and my life for a little man. Maggie knew you better than I did. She said, "Is he big enough to stand it?" I said you were, but you're not. You're a little man. You've cheated me . . . I'm ten times the man you are. You've charm, a sort of weak, helpless charm; that's all you have . . . . because you're small, you can't contain, you can't imagine a love that's a consuming fire . . . . You have loved me, Henry, but never as I have loved you. I wanted you all to myself, all your love, all your friendship, all your companionship. I couldn't share you with anyone, not even with your own daughter.

III *Producer and Lecturer in America*

It was quite the literary vogue during the booming 1920's for European authors to come to the United States as lecturers at schools, universities, and clubs of various kinds. Robinson, already an experienced traveler in the United States and Canada while managing the Abbey Company on their extensive tours, was booked in the fall of 1928 to lecture in the larger eastern cities on three subjects: the history of the Abbey, playmaking, and Irish poetry. During his stay of three months, he did not make much money; in fact, at the advice of some of his American friends he gambled a little on the stock market and lost his investment. But, unlike his previous visits when he had to cope with the day-by-day problems and affairs of the Abbey Company, he greatly enjoyed himself this time, attending plays and in general savoring the unique qualities of American life that he liked.

Robinson again returned to the United States from Ireland in the spring of 1930, six months after directing at the Abbey his experimental play, *Ever the Twain,* derived from his experiences on his previous American lecture tour and from his knowledge of American cultural life. On this occasion he served as a visiting guest producer and professor for brief periods at several American universities. First, he spent a few weeks at Amherst College directing *The Playboy;* then he continued his itinerary with productions of *The Round Table* at the Carnegie Institute of Technology and of *The Whiteheaded Boy* at the University of Michigan in May.

At the invitation of Professor Harold G. Merriam, Chairman of the Department of English at the University of Montana, Robinson taught a summer school class at the Missoula campus. Robinson soon became a warm personal friend of Professor Merriam, whom he later mentioned in his small book on the Abbey, *Pictures in a Theatre.* While at Missoula, Robinson fell much in love with the surrounding countryside, writes Professor Merriam, especially with the Bitterroot Valley and with the blue of the Sapphire Range. He respected Robinson as "a quiet and deliberate worker both in the classroom and when producing a play. He used no flurry of the half-frantic director, no loud speaking dictatorial tone." [14]

Robinson's academic schedule included daily lectures about the Irish theatre, seminars on playwriting on alternate mornings, and rehearsals every evening. At the beginning of his course on the history of the Abbey he was, he said, apprehensive lest he would not have enough content to talk about: "I rather quailed at the idea of spreading the history of our theatre over thirty lectures but by bringing in a great deal of Irish history as a background I found thirty were not too many." [15]

A month prior to his next journey to America, Robinson on September 8, 1931, in London, married Dorothy Travers Smith, daughter of a prominent Dublin doctor and granddaughter of the noted Trinity scholar Edward Dowden. A witty and talented artist, she was for many years the leading scene designer at the Abbey. She first met her husband at one of the sociable "At homes" that her mother frequently held. The Robinsons had no children.

When the Abbey Company revisited the United States and Canada in October after being away from there for eighteen years, Robinson and his wife agreed to make this tour their honeymoon. Robinson, in the role of advance lecturer for the Company, and his wife traveled from coast to coast and from Calgary down to Florida. On these journeys Robinson was able to observe the marked improvement that had come over the plays of the American theatre, thanks largely to the leadership of American universities and colleges. He was delighted that they were distinctly American and not, as heretofore, copies of English drawing room comedies or imitations derived from the stock formulas of the French well-made plays. This transformation Robinson attributed to the influence of the earlier visits of the Abbey players: "Our Irish plays had taught American playwrights that there was American material lying ready to hand, material which was germane to American soil and no other." [16] Indeed, no less a playwright than Eugene O'Neill, who was among the faithful minority that watched the Irish plays and players, confirms Robinson's opinions: "It was seeing the Irish players that gave me a glimpse of my opportunity." [17]

IV *American Influences*

Some of Robinson's previous plays had disclosed a nascent interest in dramatic experimentation. In *The Round Table*, as noted previously, he introduced the mysterious bells that Daisy heard, symbolizing an enchanting far-off region where one could be free from the daily responsibilities of life; in *The Dreamers*, as he mentioned in its preface, he sought to interweave fact and fancy. Robinson's desire for variety in his dramatic techniques was more consciously fulfilled in two plays, penned within a period of five years of each other: *Ever the Twain* in 1929 and *Church Street* in 1934. The former, acted at the Abbey under his direction on October 8, celebrated his twenty-first anniversary as a playwright. Afterwards a joyful Yeats wrote to Olivia Shake-

speare: "Lennox's play is a very great success, house packed." [18]
The innovations in *Ever the Twain*, written shortly after Robinson's return from his lecture tour in the United States in 1928, disclose his indebtedness to Eugene O'Neill. As an admirer of O'Neill's experiments in the theatre, Robinson had introduced some of O'Neill's plays to Dublin audiences, including a first production at the Abbey of *The Emperor Jones* early in 1927. Robinson later paid tribute to O'Neill when he proposed him as one of the associates of the Irish Academy of Letters.

O'Neill uses expressionism to unveil the hidden forces beneath the surface of life. To capture the mood of futility created by man's subjection to the machine in the modern age, O'Neill treats his characters as mere puppets without wills of their own. Robinson, too, as a means of satirizing the standardization of certain features of American life, incorporates a scene where people behave like robots. Writing to his friend Dean Curtis Canfield of the Yale School of Drama about *Ever the Twain*, Robinson, however, pointed out, "in spite of my play, I love the States." [19]

The plot in this good-natured comedy of manners is slight, and it has no focal or central figure. The ultimate fate of each individual in the play is left unresolved; even a quite briefly sketched love affair is not completed. Moreover, since the author's characterizing is somewhat stilted and lacking in dramatic action, one can only assume that he is mainly concerned with creating an atmosphere. This he does in stressing the ambivalent relationships between the New and Old Worlds. The younger generation in the United States is depicted as fighting against European influence and aspiring to have a soul of its own. Young America is epitomized in the character of Carl Svenson, an energetic Swedish-American farmer, who proudly argues that his lineage is just as honorable as that of a visiting English novelist, Chesterfield Wragsdale:

Carl   What's your background?

Wragsdale   Generations of English men and women stretching back for hundreds of years. Never very distinguished, but always a tradition of culture and decent living, old furniture, old books, an unbroken heritage handed down from generation to generation, gradually a patina, a tradition.

Carl   I can beat you for tradition. I'm a farmer, so's my dad, so's my grand-dad and back as far as you care to count . . . right back to the garden of Eden I guess. He came out here, my grand-dad did and his three brothers, straight from a farm in Sweden, straight to the land here. They cleaned it, built a shack, got a few hogs, a patch of corn, then more hogs, more corn, then they knocked down the shacks and built themselves houses. Tradition! Those farms are pure Svenson. Svenson muscle and Svenson sweat have gone to the making of every blessed acre of them. We've married there, bred there, died there, and you've the nerve to tell me we've neither atmosphere nor tradition.

Wragsdale   It's different.

Carl   Sure it's different, it's America. You won't admit that we've got a soul to call our own, we're only some kind of ignorant country cousins to you, we've got to show you that we're just as different from you as an oak tree is from an automobile . . . . You only respect the fellow who knocks you down. Look at Ireland, she was a sort of comic strip in a newspaper, until she bested you.

Set in opposition to Carl is another kind of American, Nicholas Brice. His opinions and impressions of the United States suggest that Robinson probably modeled this character after the American novelist, Henry James, whose novels the playwright valued highly. Brice, who belongs to a generation able to find in European culture much of satisfying import, considers himself European in taste and thought. He proposes to retire from a thriving law practice and then to leave what to him is a noisy, brash United States. But, before going, he prophesies about its cultural prospects:

Nicholas   I shock you I think. I shock most of my American friends. They don't hold with anyone who just idles, who's just out to enjoy life.

Carl   Life's not meant just to be enjoyed. It's . . . I don't suppose I've got any right to say these things to you, Mr. Brice—but it seems to me it's kind of disloyal of you to quit. It makes out that America's not good enough for you.

Nicholas   It isn't. That's the whole truth of the matter. I'm European, all my tastes, all my thoughts are European, every year I live here I see the country swinging west, turning in on itself. Every old book, every old master you buy stamps you as being non-European; you buy them as curiosities, as examples of a civilization not your own. I want to live in a country where these things are taken for granted.

Carl   You could hang on and help make it good enough.

Nicholas   And you'll work and work and grow richer and richer.

Carl   I aim at that.

Nicholas   That's just where we differ. I don't believe that the States will be fit to live in till people like you are glutted with work and money, till you've made so many dollars you just get sick and start to idle. But that's for your son—or your son's son. It won't come in my time, so I'm going to quit.

Incidental to this contrast of tastes and philosophies the author casts a series of satirical barbs against both worlds. The international lecturers, among them a young Irish poet who brings condensed culture to the United States, are shown to be just as conscious of money as of art. The author, too, gives evidence that he has faith in the sincerity and goals of young Americans, yet he does not spare from severe criticism the middle-class, middle-aged clubwomen who slavishly mouth the current clichés about art. Their pseudo-appreciation offers the playwright scope for experimenting with expressionistic techniques to mimic their automatic, unthinking mumbo jumbo.

A casual remark of one of the Americans, a very minor character, at the final curtain, perhaps, best sums up the point of the play: "We're different you see. Just blamed different. That's saying everything. Get me, different. Yes sir, and always will be."

V   *The Significance of* Church Street

Robinson's long one act play, *Church Street*, represents one of the most significant of all his works, principally because of what it acknowledged about his own artistic quandaries—quandaries also relevant to his fellow Irish playwrights. Written between December, 1933, and March, 1934, partly in Dublin, partly in Arles, Robinson staged *Church Street* at the Abbey on May 21, 1934, with a distinguished cast including all of the famous Abbey actors.

After almost twenty years of looking beyond the Irish scene to extend the range of his literary vistas, the playwright now reaches a decisive point in his career. Robinson believes it necessary to question the road he had taken in the past, to reexamine his inclinations and his aims as a writer, and to make a fresh appraisal of what direction his work in the Irish theatre should take.

The flash of patriotic insight that sparked him into writing for the Irish theatre, after his first seeing *Kathleen ni Houlihan* and the Abbey players at the Cork Opera House in 1907, once more exerts its sway upon his subconscious and stimulates a similar awakening. Just as then, this compelling vision induces him to reflect that "My material, the stone I must chisel and fashion was the stone on the hillside outside my door; the people I must write about, the only people I could write about must be my family and my friends round the fireside, the people I met and talked with on the road or in the haggard. . . . I try to express this in a play called *Church Street,* where a young playwright not unlike myself takes the subject for his play from a life outside his knowledge, ignoring the material that lives to his hand, blood of his blood, flesh of his flesh." [20]

But another inner voice warns Robinson that it would be unwise to go back to the manner of his earlier years. Trying to resolve his artistic problem, he then proposes a compromise. Why not take his subject matter from Irish character and life and superimpose upon it the latest experimental ideas and methods of the international theatre. As a consequence, in writing *Church Street* he not only falls back upon his memories of people he once knew in Kinsale, but also utilizes the technique of Pirandello whose work in "dramatizing the intellect" he had extolled at the opening of the experimental Peacock Theatre.

One of the intellectual problems engrossing the mind of Pirandello was the mystery of reality. His preoccupation obtained imaginative outlets in his dramas depicting the evolution of a character in an author's mind. In the best known of these, *Six Characters in Search of an Author,* Pirandello disavowed the belief held by many that the author's will controls his characters: that they are mere marionettes dancing at his beck and call. What really happens, he contended, is that a character at birth takes on its own life and soon acquires an individualism of its own beyond the control of its author.

In *Church Street* Robinson adapts these subjective premises of Pirandello to his own ends in dramatizing a first-rate topic: that tragedy, abortive love, frustration, and hunger can exist in the common daily life of people, but the casual observer will pay little or no heed to these realities. Robinson also bares the operations of a writer's mind on the stage before his audience as he constructs his play about an incomplete play. At the same time, he acknowledges that far-off places, although exotically enticing, are not so rich for dramatic inspiration as one might assume; home fields can be far more fertile when properly cultivated.

Hugh Riordan, a discontented and perplexed young dramatist who has a flair for writing comedies, can see no hope anywhere for his future as an author. His London productions have been poorly received, a fact that Robinson uses as a point of irony against himself; for *All's Over Then?* had previously been a failure in London. Hugh's plays deal with areas of life about which he knows little, hence their lack of success. Frustrated, he comes back to Ireland to his father's comfortable home in Knock, where he expects to be at peace and to collect ideas for his writing. There, though, the dullness and the monotony of small town society temporarily blight his prospects until his elderly Aunt Moll, a keen and wise observer of the local scene, takes an interest in his problems as an artist. After listening to his complaints, she assumes the role of Hugh's other self, performing as his conscience, guide, and catalyst.

Knock has an abundance of life, Aunt Moll claims, if only Hugh will open his eyes to it. Then, as the guests assemble for his mother's dinner party, Aunt Moll tells him that tragedy and comedy lie before him among these plain and presumably ordinary people, and that tragedy is in the ascendant. His aunt alludes to the dramatic possibilities inherent in Miss Pettigrew and her sister, formerly in better circumstances but now almost starving on a very meager allowance; in Hugh's previous love, Honor Bewley, once a gay, vibrant girl, but aging before her time because of a broken heart; in Jim Daly, a Catholic medical student, and in Sallie Long, the daughter of a Protestant minister, who love each other dearly but are prevented from marrying because of their religious beliefs. In addition, grave complications are hinted at for Sallie in a pending operation in London.

Each of these potentialities is sharply and rapidly etched. Each also contains within its brief limits the central idea of the play; still, the conciseness of each episode prevents one from making full acquaintance with any of the characters. In fine, Robinson attempts too much by bringing in so many incidents under one grouping, even though he shows quite skillful craftsmanship in fusing the disconnected scenes.

The briefing of Hugh's aunt alerts him to the fact that his imagination was dormant and that there is viable dramatic life among the guests in need of shaping. He ponders: "But it's inevitable, or is it? Is it all in my own mind or must—or must it happen? Am I shaping events or are they shaping me? Is it all predestined? Will you all stand by, please. I'll summon you as I need you. I must see them on the stage as I see them in my mind." Hugh then goes on to work out his ideas on stage, organizing them in separate vignettes; the tragedy in the lives of the two sisters and in the dissonances between Sallie and Jim receives most of his attention. Sallie conceives Jim's child and has to go to an abortionist in London for an operation which leads to her death.

Another Pirandellian feature is perceptible in Robinson's treatment of the overlapping nature of fiction and reality. In his stage directions describing the first entrance of the dinner guests, Robinson specifies that their arrival should be lifelike: "All come in awkwardly, in a bunch, and having got in, don't quite know what to do with themselves." Yet the imagined exits and entrances of Hugh's characters later in his embryo play are carefully arranged to build up a dramatic climax. Robinson thereby unveils the process of artistic selection that makes order out of the disorder of daily events to create the fictional life that Pirandello maintained had more reality than life itself.

So absorbed, however, does Robinson become in portraying the two Pettigrew sisters that he rounds out *Church Street* with a puzzling finale. The vividness of Hugh's fictional world makes him wonder if he is outside the boundaries of reality. For a moment Hugh drops his role of creator and asks the real Miss Pettigrew about the contents of her bag to see if she is carrying out food from his mother's table to satisfy her hunger when she reaches home. Perhaps fancy is really fact after all. But before one gets an opportunity to explore further this interesting speculation, the play ends.

VI   *Adaptions*

Robinson sought another outlet for testing and extending his skills as a theatrical craftsman by adapting for the modern theatre the works of other writers. The first of these was an amusing *tour de force, The Critic,* in which Robinson transfers the setting and period of Sheridan's famous play to Dublin of the late 1920's. Apparently Robinson toyed with the idea at the outset, because, in the first of the two editions now in the Abbey Theatre's library of plays, he only slightly altered Sheridan's original. But the comic possibilities inherent in bringing that play up to date must have struck Robinson's fancy, for, in his second attempt, he made considerable changes in Sheridan's first act and lesser ones in the other two acts.

On the opening night at the Abbey on January 6, 1931, as a gracious bow to the inspirer of his play, Robinson came on stage and shook hands with "Sheridan," acted by one of the cast. To brief his audience further, Robinson also included in the program notes an explanatory prologue:

No apology is necessary for rewriting *The Critic* and bringing it up to date. When it was written, its first act was very topical and much of its humour in that act is derived from the fact that it mentioned by name contemporary persons, newspapers and events. For instance, when on the play's first night (October 29, 1779) Puff spoke of the actors Dodd and Palmer, he spoke of the creators of the parts of his Benjamin Backbite and Joseph Surface and in praising the King—the original Sir Peter Teazle—he praised himself . . . it is in the spirit of Sheridan's play to make the actor playing Puff's part praise his fellow players and himself. Of course, the ridiculous inner play, 'The Spanish Armada,' is left unaltered. The 'yon battlements' style of drama is still being written, worse luck; it is my misfortune to have read many such plays each twelve months.[21]

In the first act, in which most of the play's alterations occur, the author proffers a pleasantly satirical litany involving many topical facets of life in Dublin—artistic, political, and social. Dangle sets the scene as he asks his wife for a copy of the *Daily Express* to read the Irish theatre notes. With the entrance of Sneer, Puff, and Plagiary, an amusing panoramic review of notable Dublin personalities and their activities begins: adverse trade balances; the debatable topic of compulsory Irish; drama critics attacking the Abbey; the Drama League; "peasant" plays; lunching or drinking at fashionable Dublin cafes; jealous authors charging Abbey directors with plagiarizing plots of rejected plays. Each item is subjected to mild ridicule, and the play moves blithely on to its finish. For the finale, the original sea fight becomes a ballet depicting the Shannon Hydroelectric Scheme, one of the Irish government's projects for modernizing the country.

The calm of Ireland's neutrality during World War II was briefly disturbed through Robinson's next adaptation, Maupassant's novelette *Boule de Suif* as *Roly Poly*. Much of this drama's interest stems from the spectacular hubbub created in Dublin because of the play's topicality in a country attempting very objectively and carefully to maintain its neutrality in a warring world. Increasing the difficulties of the director, Hilton Edwards, Robinson modernized his story which he began as a period piece about the Franco-Prussian War. Regardless of Edward's protests that the play lost more than it gained by this change, Robinson insisted that Edwards stage this modern version or none at all. The lure of novelty and the dramatic possibilities of the script compelled Edwards to reconsider it. Nor, as he smilingly added, "could he ignore the fact that a motor bus was easier to handle upon the stage than a diligence with a horse." [22]

After the opening night on November 19, 1940, at the Gate Theatre, *Roly Poly*—as a reminder that history kept repeating itself—was too much to bear for the susceptibilities of the ambassadors from the two opposing nations in the bloody conflict raging beyond Ireland's shores. Officials of both the French and German legations in Dublin angrily complained that Maupassant's picture of the debasing influence of the Franco-Prussian War on both peoples was too harrowing for their war-torn nerves. Each nation felt that its name suffered at the expense of the other. The Germans, for instance, protested at Roly Poly's scornful attitude when she threw a basket of bread at a German sentry. At any rate, representatives of both legations filed protests with the Irish Department of External Affairs, claiming that Robinson's play violated Irish neutrality.

Edwards was then called before a minister of the Irish government and ordered to withdraw *Roly Poly* on the grounds that it was obscene. The inaccuracy of this charge and the government's ban prohibiting public explanation of his artistic aims aroused his ire. He consulted with Robinson, who reminded him about the previous victories of Yeats, Lady Gregory, and himself against governmental control. So they agreed to put the play on at least once more.

Prior to the second night's performance the Department of Justice used the wartime Emergency Powers Act to remove all advertisements about *Roly Poly,* replacing them with the government's explanatory notices. That night intense excitement reigned on both sides of the curtains. A few minutes before the play began for an overflow audience which included one minister of the government, an agent of the Ministry of Justice telephoned. He warned that if *Roly Poly* went on, the patent of the theatre would be cancelled. Coinciding with the call, two detectives came backstage to enforce the government's regulations.

Without delay the two producers, Hilton Edwards and Micheál MacLiammoir, pulled aside the curtains, and Edwards announced that there were two reasons, both backstage, preventing them from staging *Roly Poly* that night. After apologizing to the audience, MacLiammoir explained to them that they would get their money back at the box office.

Just as the stunned members of the audience began to move from their seats, Robinson, observing all from the wings, dramatically walked to the center of the stage. Blinking in the glare of the spotlights, he languorously raised his long arms and in his high pitched voice, emotionally cried out, "Keep your seats! I have bought out the house! You are my guests! The show will go on!" [23] Edwards, quite aware that Irish writers have rather limited means and that the financial loss would be mainly his worry, was heard to comment, "With what?" [24]

Robinson's offer stirred a now fascinated house, and all agreed to stay with the lone exception of the government minister. A splendid cast, not to be outdone, acted as if inspired and gave an exceptional performance. As the final curtain was about to fall, the still tensed audience rose to give the actors a memorable ovation. An audience spokesman later came on stage to say that no one wanted a refund, and that the money should be used for a relief fund for the relatives of those lost in a drowning fatality off the west coast of Ireland. Two days after the closing of *Roly Poly,* the excitement still had not died down for the playwright;

a member of the French Legation called on him and stiffly informed him that the French Minister wished to fight a duel in defense of the honor of France.

To adapt Maupassant's story for the stage, Robinson selects twelve short episodes from it; and the result affords a specimen of Robinson's craftsmanship in the theatre—even if the original is more effective as a piece of literature. Robinson's main difficulties of construction apparently lay in breathing more life into Maupassant's surface characters and in generating dramatic tension for a tale of limited action. To do so, however, Robinson was obliged to introduce considerable explanatory matter, which detracts from the play's effectiveness. Granted that Roly Poly is fairly clearly drawn, the remaining characters are much too sketchy to know intimately. Robinson, too, attempted to lessen the acid quality in Maupassant's work by portraying Roly as more romantic and glamorous than her prototype, Boule.

Towards the end of Robinson's life, the theatre was too much in his veins to let him rest. Although recuperating from a heart attack, he undertook an adaption of Turgenev's *Fathers and Sons* and consulted with his playwright friend Miss Deevy about sundry technical problems of their craft. In the throes of writing the first act, he asked her, "How should I fill up the space at the end? I want the mother to get off before the curtain, as she has to have time to change for the next scene and maybe my hand has lost its cunning." [25] Robinson eventually completed this play a short time before his death, but it was neither produced nor published.

In perspective, this phase of Robinson's contributions to the theatre can be considered as entertaining and diverting but as generally disappointing. His increasing sophistication evident in the widened scope of his dramatic vision and his appealing skill in probing the secrets of the human heart are offset by a tendency towards an uncertain and sometimes even somewhat superficial treatment of his material. Finally, although Robinson's search for more extensive theatrical horizons was not successful—as he himself admitted in *Church Street*—he well deserves, nonetheless, to be commended for his enterprising pioneering endeavors to add an international flavor to the Irish drama.

[136]

CHAPTER 6

The Magnetic "Irish Thing"

THE most subtle and in many ways the most influential of all the forces at play upon Robinson's art, mind, and senses was the subconscious magnetism of what he termed "this strange Irish thing, the commanding force in my life." Nowhere did Robinson specifically call this "Irish thing" patriotism or love of country. Thus he implied that it represented dedication to an ideal deeper and more inclusive than political or social goals, to an ideal also incorporating devotion to art, ideas, and the realm of the spirit. He once described it as:

the thing vague and yet luminous which started to take shape and to glow as soon as I was old enough to have a mind and a judgement of my own. Women and men I grew to know, or read of in history suffered and died for this thing. I gave nothing, suffered nothing, in fact received much from it. Through the years it still glows, after years— some of disappointment—it is still not possible for me to think of any life apart from it. . . .[1]

The "Irish thing" had lain almost dormant through the years of Robinson's quest for more varied literary experiences. But in the period between 1926 and 1929—when he was in the middle of his exploratory, experimental phase—one can locate the initial causes for the resurgence of the "Irish thing." During those years he broke the chain of his cosmopolitan creations when he penned two dramas, *The Big House* and *The Far-Off Hills*, both having their inspiration in the warp and woof of Irish life. Of these, *The Far-Off Hills*, a comedy based on the same provincial country town background as that of *The Whiteheaded Boy*, was to become the second most successful of his plays.

The admiration this comedy won and the subsequent popularity it acquired apparently planted a certain amount of doubt and indecision in the playwright's mind regarding the wisdom of continuing with his cosmopolitan interests. His confusion about his bearings at this time was increased further by the fact that, although he had obtained his material for *The Far-Off Hills* from Irish life, he, as will be seen later, had derived its central idea from his experiences with the Continental plays of the Drama League.

The perplexing nature of the problem he faced caused Robinson probably to ponder thus to himself: the dramatic material that spreads before me in my native country develops in me a sense of ease and sympathetic understanding whereby I can write interestingly and well. What is more, the non-Irish sources I have tapped for ideas have turned out unsuccessful dramatically; they have failed to build up that satisfying public appreciation so encouraging to an artist. Could it be that the genre that suits me best is comedy based on Irish characters I know quite intimately?

But these promptings of his instincts were apparently merely temporary ones, for he decided to suppress their attraction. Instead, he saw fit to renew his efforts to satisfy his urbane, cosmopolitan tastes; and so, in the period extending from 1929 to 1932, his plays have little or nothing especially Irish about them. Not until one comes to the excellently received *Drama at Inish,* a farce inspired by his observations of the Irish theatre, does one observe once again the pull of the Irish magnet—"the Irish thing"—exerting its control over him. This was an important stage in his literary career, for the success of this farce led to a dramatized confession of his artistic difficulties as an Irish writer in the soul-searching *Church Street* produced in the following year, 1934.

I *The "Big House" Theme*

That the unique role of the "Big House" in Ireland should act as a special magnet drawing Robinson back to a reexamination of Irish life is understandable. Like many another Anglo-Irish writer before him, Robinson was attracted by the appeal of what Daniel Corkery classified as the leading theme in Anglo-Irish literature, the decline and fall of the "Big House." [2]

Synge had already noticed its possibilities when he wrote in his book of travel memoirs, *In Wicklow and West Kerry:* ". . . if a playwright chose to go through the Irish country houses he would find material, it is very likely, for many gloomy plays that would turn on the dying of these old families." [3] Yeats, too, had deplored the decay of the large estates and the decline of the landowning class; to him the "Big House" represented the esteemed guardian of aristocratic traditions "where passion and precision have been one." Indeed, in *Purgatory*, he had declared it "a capital offence" to destroy these houses where great men had lived out their lives.

Who, then, were the people of the "Big House"? Racially they represented a mixing, over many generations, of two bloods, Irish and English. In religion they were chiefly Protestant in a country predominantly Catholic; and quite frequently their schooling was received in England.[4] From their educational training and their religious outlook, they found themselves drawn towards England. Yet, at the same time, despite this pull, their native land brought deeper, stronger forces to bear on their consciousness. In fine, Ireland—as Elizabeth Bowen, herself a product of the "Big House" once explained—had worked on them through their senses, their nerves, and their loves.

Robinson put to advantage his own experience of having lived in one of the "Big Houses," at the estate of the O'Briens of Cahirmoyle, but it was not until several years after he had left their home that the time spent there bore fruit. One evening, driving home to Dublin after a visit to "Wicklow," he saw in the distance a semideserted "Big House." Its air of mystery caught his fancy; [5] these thoughts came to him: "Perhaps . . . in that Georgian house or sham Gothic castle there remained an old father and mother and a couple of aged daughters. The house was too large for their needs or too large for their purse and what reason was there for clinging to it? Meanwhile the house was too full of memories of past greatness, too full of memories of boys who had shot rabbits in the long summer evenings. . . ." [6] The sequel to such reflection, he continued, was that "I fell into a reverie and spoke no word until we reached home. A play of mine was born then. I called it *The Big House*, and if anyone cares to read it, they will find in it a picture of that lovely woman, Mary Spring Rice." [7]

Against the backdrop of Ireland's intense struggle for freedom which was gathering momentum during and after World War I, the playwright in four scenes sets the drama of the life of one of these "Big Houses," symbolizing a declining tradition and a disintegrating order. Robinson again reflects Yeats's views, for he, too, finds this class a source of admiration and regrets its loss; but, at the same time, he makes a compromise by showing himself in sympathy with the aspirations of a changing Ireland.

The Alcock family has had its family seat in Ballydonal House in County Cork for generations. Not typical of the Anglo-Irish landlord class, who through the years had shown a tendency to deteriorate culturally and mentally, the Alcocks feel themselves a protest against this type, which, in the play is exemplified by Vandaleur O'Neill, a loutish, penniless member of a once prominent but now decadent Anglo-Irish family.

On Armistice Day, November, 1918, the Alcocks have a small celebration to toast the war's ending and to greet the anxiously anticipated return of Ulick, their son. Captain Despard, an English officer back from the front, fell in love with Kate, the Alcock's only daughter, while she was visiting London. He calls on her at Ballydonal House, proposes to her, and suggests that she leave Ireland to begin life with him in England. She discourages his offer because Ballydonal and Irish life have too deeply rooted an appeal for her. She and her brother Ulick share the same dream of maintaining the influence of the "Big House" tradition among the Irish people. Her brother means so much to her that she even imagines that she sees his spirit haunting the house. This vision becomes a bad omen, for, in the middle of the celebration, news arrives of Ulick's death in the war.

The second scene switches to the house in 1921, a year of bloodshed and brutality in Ireland, when the hated "Black and Tans" roamed the land. Kate's attempts to bridge the gap between herself and her Irish-Catholic neighbors are not very rewarding; worse still, the more Kate tries, the more she finds herself rebuffed. Instinctively she hits on the core of her problem after she goes to pay her respects at the wake of her former maid who had been shot by the avenging "Black and Tans." So greatly are nationality and religion interlocked that she feels she does not quite belong despite her good intentions:

Kate   There I was in that cottage with the neighbours and Father Doyle and Doctor Hennessy and I knew Maggie better than any of them, and I—I was an outsider . . . different, away from them.

The Magnetic "Irish Thing"

Alcock When death is in question one feels, of course, that religion makes such a difference.

Kate Yes, there was religion to make me feel outside but lots of other things too; education, I suppose, and tradition and—and everything that makes me me and them them. Between us and them, like the people in the Bible, there was "a great gulf fixed."

Alcock I know no one who has made less of the gulf than you, Kitty. Your democracy shocks your mother. . . .

Kate I've known the people in the village all my life. I've worked with them, quarrelled with them, loved them, but at the end of it all I find myself—just different.

Alcock Maybe it's right we should be different.

Kate How can it be right? I want to be the same.

Alcock You'll never be that.

Kate Why not?

Alcock It will be always "them" and "us."

Upon joining the "Tans" as an officer, Despard returns drunk to the scene of his earlier friendships; and his new role of avenger is distasteful to him. Kate again repulses him; then, in a melodramatic finale to the scene, Despard fires his gun at the imaginary voice of Ulick mocking him from outside the window.

Two years elapse and the decadent O'Neills, who fled Ireland when their castle was burned in the Anglo-Irish war, ironically enough have acquired social and economic prestige in England. Kate, on the other hand, has tried working in London, but she discovers that she is lonely and out of place there. After a while she returns home only to learn that the young Republicans in the Civil War have chosen her home for burning as a reprisal for the actions of the governing Free State Party. The "Irregulars" order the Alcocks out of their home and burn most of their possessions. Yet, at the end of the long trail of discouragement and disintegration, only the alert and realistic Kate can achieve an efficacious purgation and cleansing of her soul in this last grim rebuff. In her defiance she attains a renascence of spirit when quoting Yeats's exortation, "Ireland is not more theirs than ours, we must glory in our difference, be as proud of it as they are of theirs." [8]

Alcock   "They," "us!" Do you remember, Kate, the evening after Maggie Leahy was shot?

Kate   Yes. But now I don't want to give up the "they" and "us." I glory in it. I was wrong, we were all wrong in trying to find a common platform, in pretending we weren't different from every Pat and Mick in the village. . . . We were ashamed of everything, ashamed of our birth, ashamed of our good religion, ashamed that we dined in the evenings and that we dressed for dinner, and, after all, our shame didn't save us or we wouldn't be sitting here in the remnants of our furniture.

Alcock   And what can save you now, it's too late?

Kate   If it was too late they wouldn't have bothered to burn us; they don't think it is too late so why should we? They're afraid of us still.

Mrs. Alcock   We do look formidable, don't we?

Kate   We are formidable if we care to make ourselves so, if we give up our poor attempt to pretend we're not different. We must glory in our difference, be as proud of it as they are of theirs . . . . because we're what we are. Ireland is not more theirs than ours.

Born and reared in England, Mrs. Alcock has never felt herself quite at home in Ireland, even after a twenty-year residence. She thinks the burning of their home should be a warning to them that it is time for the family to leave Ireland for good. Her husband, the most tragic character in the drama, perceives that he has no other choice despite all his sincere efforts to be of service to the community and to identify himself with local causes. His tragedy lies in his inability ever really to understand the people of his environment.

Only Kate is willing to commence a new life in Ballydonal House. The memories of Ulick and their combined dreams are everywhere for her in the house, and they revitalize her determination and hope. As the final curtain falls, she beholds once again the consoling vision of Ulick:

Ulick. . . . (She turns to the summer house and speaks softly) Ulick! Are you there? (Her face lights up.) Oh, my dear, you've come

to me again, after all these years. . . . And you're smiling, so I'm
right, it's what you'd have done . . . (A pause, she seems to listen to
someone talking) Yes . . . Yes . . . So—kiss me, my dear. (She
raises her face as if she were being kissed, she closes her eyes).

This play, first performed under Robinson's direction at the
Abbey on September 6, 1926, does duty as a supplement to
O'Casey's *Juno and the Paycock* (1924) and *The Plough and the
Stars* (1926). It brings to view a new side to the tragedy inherent in the doleful years of the Anglo-Irish War and the Civil
War. Instead of being shown how the life of the tenement dwell-
ers is affected by those tumultuous times, one is now made
aware of their telling consequences upon the life of the Ascendancy. Robinson's approach is less emotional, more objective, than
O'Casey's in his attempt to clarify a problem; yet, at the same
time one cannot help but feel, despite the superb dialogue,
that the characters in *The Big House* lack true depth. Even
though Robinson shows considerable care to search deeply into
their inner personalities, they seem also to be merely sounding
boards for the author's opinions of the position of this order in
the evolving Irish scene. His sociological analysis of this segment of Irish life would appear to be more important to him than
his shaping of the drama flowing from the nuances of the Ascendancy character. His last act demonstrates once again that lack of
finality which takes away from the merits of so many of his plays.
The drama, as a whole, displays also the playwright's melodramatic inclinations that tempt and lead him away from his
theme.
Another facet of Robinson's interest in the "Big House" theme
is dramatized in his comedy, *When Lovely Woman*,[9] in which he
depicts the decline of the stately homes of the English aristocracy
through financial losses and through failure to propagate. It represents also the playwright's last and somewhat halfhearted sally
outside Ireland to garner substance for his plays. Before its unsuccessful production at the Gate Theatre on August 18, 1936,
some discouraging prospects arose. First of all, the Abbey directors refused the play because they considered it too blasé in
tone and not suitable for Abbey requirements. Then the opening
night was postponed for four days because the leading actress
withdrew at the last moment.[10]

But these setbacks merely serve as fitting omens for what is possibly one of the least satisfactory of all Robinson's plays. He seems to have wearied of his basic idea before he had advanced as far as his second act. Mrs. Faithful Jagoe, portrayed at the outset as his central figure, fails to give much cohesion to what appears in the end to be merely a sequence of episodes. In the somewhat implausible plot, this odd and imperious woman is left a rich widow from her husband's stock market investments in the United States. She dedicates herself to preserving the aristocratic traditions and families of England and to spending her money and time in carrying out her aims. She also devotes herself to the vexations and trials of aristocratic lovers who are involved in premarital affairs. To these couples she grants financial allotments to encourage them to legalize their position by marriage.

The Honorable John Warrenden, potential heir to the estate of his father, Lord Broom, and Sylvia Buchan are such a pair; they have been living together but have not formalized their relationship. Sylvia is the daughter of a mere merchant. For this reason, she does not merit approval of Mrs. Jagoe, who wants a more aristocratic woman to become John's wife. Sylvia thinks otherwise; she deems that her "design-for-living" with John is satisfactory enough without legalization or bowing to Mrs. Jagoe's wishes.

The sly Sylvia attempts to sidetrack her equally self-willed and shrewd opponent, so she calls her attention to another member of the upper classes who could use financial backing to get married. Sylvia recommends Maurice Corrigan, a young and comparatively poor Irish landlord with a beautiful but rotting mansion and a neglected estate in the west of Ireland. Through Maurice, Robinson gives the drama an Irish touch—one suggesting that Robinson was vacillating between his two horizons, the Irish and non-Irish worlds.

Sylvia assumes that Mrs. Jagoe is only interested in helping the immoral ones; and, knowing that Maurice is relatively blameless, she maps out her schemes to loosen Mrs. Jagoe's purse strings. In reality, however, Mrs. Jagoe aids financially both moral and immoral couples—if they have aristocratic pedigrees. From this confusion arises whatever comedy exists in the play. Sylvia dangles the glamour and romance of Maurice's Irish estate before the susceptible widow, as the opening move in her plan. Before long, Sylvia's subtle strategy leads Mrs. Jagoe to grant Maurice the money he needs for marriage. For the rest of her life, Mrs. Jagoe will spend half of each year in England and the other half on Maurice's Irish estate which she is determined to restore to its former attractiveness. John Warrenden, in the last moments of the play, learns that by his father's death he has succeeded to the family title and property.

Eleven years elapsed before Robinson brought out what may be accounted as his sequel and corollary to *The Big House.* Called *Killycreggs in Twilight,* it had its first showing at the Abbey on April 19, 1937. One can obtain a glimpse of its birth pangs from Robinson's dedication of it to two American writers: "The first and second acts of this play to Ellen and Philip Barry . . . in whose villa at Cannes this play was imagined last February . . . the last act in memory of Edith Wharton, who spurred me to write it in a day in her lovely chateau at Hyeres."

In a somewhat unconvincing drama jarred out of focus by the widening gap between his exaggeration on the one hand and his understatement on the other, Robinson again places the people of the "Big House" at a decisive point in their career. Will they make a compromise with the new Ireland, or will they retire from the battlefield defeated?

An omnipresent rot has set in on the de Lury family, owners of Killycreggs House, Connemara. The traditions of the family have been to send the eldest boy off to school or to the Army in England; to allow the remaining males to drift into a pleasantly idle but boring existence; and to leave the daughters without much education. The changes created by the regenerative forces in Ireland have intensified the atmosphere of decay, turning Killycreggs into a second "Cherry Orchard." Of the two de Lury sisters, Judith and Kit, the former determines to put a stop to this downward slide into dissolution. As her contribution to solving their problem, she sells produce grown on the estate at the local marketplace; and, but for her exacting managerial ability, the finances of the house would not have remained solvent. While the plot gathers momentum, one learns that her burden is increasingly onerous for her. Under the circumstances, she seriously contemplates marrying Morgan, a prosperous, local hotel-keeper and publican, and selling the house to him for an hotel.

Her class-conscious sister, Kit, immediately resents this as a lowering of the family dignity. Equally disconcerting to her and to her visiting cousin, Dr. Pratt, is Judith's disclosure that she will have to change her religion to marry Morgan:

Judith   I wanted to keep this from you tonight, I hoped you wouldn't think of it. I'm going to become a Roman Catholic.

Kit   (utter horror in her voice) You're "turning?"

Judith   Darling, I think I'll go on saying my two or three old Protestant prayers night and morning and read the Bible father gave me on the day I was confirmed, and I don't think Father Brophy will mind— much, and I don't think God will mind at all.

Kit, nonetheless, is still sanguine about carrying on the family heritage. Owing to the uncommon traits of their young nephew, Loftus de Lury, she envisages that he will be the proper person to bring renewed vitality into Killycreggs. From the moment of his arrival on a visit, his singular charm has easily allowed him to slip into the role of seigneur of the estate. But Judith looks upon this unique de Lury personality as a weakening influence in all their lives:

Kit   Why shouldn't he be a new beginning?

Judith   (getting up, and now she's strong). Yes, why shouldn't he? That's what I want, a new de Lury. There's no room in Ireland now for places like Killycreggs, for de Lurys and their like, lounging and fishing and shooting. I wish we'd been burned out in the Troubles; I wish all our sort had been burned out. I wouldn't have behaved like that fool-girl in the play, The Big House. I would never have built Killycreggs, I'd have thanked God to be quit of it. I'm not doing this for my own sake, for my own happiness, I'm doing it for his, for Loftus's sake too. . . .

Loftus, Judith thinks, would be better off working in a job or running his own business in Dublin; but, by this time, he has fallen too much in love with the beguiling life at Killycreggs to agree with her. For a moment she reflects upon the prospect of giving up her proposed marriage with Morgan. However, Morgan tells her that Killycreggs estate is not so important to him after all; why not let the young man run it as he desires. Loftus at this critical moment makes his final appeal:

It is entailed, it is. Not by law, but by blood, by all things that matter more than words scribbled by a lawyer on a bit of parchment. This lovely house, the pictures, the ancestors that look down from the walls, that river, the— Oh! I don't want either of you to die for a hundred years, but it must come in the end to me or to my son. It's de Lury, de Lury, de Lury as long as two stones of it stick together. You're trying to do a monstrous thing, Aunt Judith; something outside nature.

As the curtain slowly falls on the third act, one is left with an impression of uncertainty; it is as if the play were unfinished. Apprehensive of Loftus's future and of his destiny in the "Big House," Judith hesitatingly remarks:

Judith   Put out the lights, Loftus. (He does so; a grey dismal light comes through the thin curtains). I don't like it, Loftus. I'm afraid, afraid.

Loftus   Silly. Silly. (The light in the hall outside is bright and he swings her into it; he shuts the door. The room is left in twilight).

II   *The Return To Laughter*

Along the somber paths that Robinson followed in his quest for untapped dramatic sources, the year 1928 loomed forth as a refreshing landmark. That year Robinson bestirred himself to listen again to the call of the "Irish thing," and, as a result, he responded with another comedy, *The Far-Off Hills*. This, his first full-length comedy of Irish life since *The Whiteheaded Boy* in 1916, had its premiere at the Abbey on October 22.

Robinson put a temporary halt to his cheerless groping chiefly through the creative satisfactions he derived from the comic spirit culled from the substance of Irish life and character. But he also gleaned much to counteract his gloomy mood from the popular, well-written, and entertaining Spanish comedies of the Quintero brothers familiar to him from his Drama League activities.

During the year prior to the production of *The Far-Off Hills*, an English translation of four of the Quinteros' plays was published.[11] Robinson quite admired them, principally the light comedy *The*

Women Have Their Way because of the brothers' conscious striving to satisfy the needs of the heart and because of their sincere note of optimistic simplicity. In all probability, the pleasant Andalusian world of the Quinteros acted as a helpful antidote for Robinson to counterbalance his prevailingly gloomy mood at this stage of his writing career. About the same time also, Robinson's Spanish tastes attracted him to the slightly sentimental approach to Catholic life evidenced in the dramas of Martinez Sierra.

The Far-Off Hills, like *The Women Have Their Way,* deals in lighthearted fashion with women's seemingly compulsive interest in marriage making. Unlike Robinson's earlier days, when the distant world of the dreamers offered seductive allure, one perceives in this domestic comedy that he regards faraway places as not so fascinating after all; more satisfaction can be gained by welcoming and savoring the reality before one.

The Clancys, a small-town family of background similar to the Geoghegans in *The Whiteheaded Boy,* are managed very firmly by the eldest daughter Marian, who aspires to be a nun some day. Her father's temporary blindness delays her final decision, because she considers that the family needs her controlling hand, especially her two vivacious and gay younger sisters. These two girls, whom Robinson delineates with benevolent amusement, think that Marian's strong control over their lives is much too irksome. To remedy this annoying situation, they devise ways and means of speeding Marian's departure for the convent. As the first stage of their "crusade" they encourage a latent romance between their widower father and Susan Tynan, an old friend of the family.

Much to their joy, these romantically minded sisters succeed in their objective; but they have misjudged the tenacity of their sister. Marian still will not come to any definite decision concerning her prospective plans to go to the convent. She believes that she would be better employed shaping their future careers.

Love again enters the household through the person of Pierce, a lively young nephew of Susan. And from the moment he pays Marian her first compliment, causing her to gaze at herself in the mirror, the audience recognizes that far-off hills are no longer green. Pierce, egged on by the two youngsters, makes love to her; he quickly wins her hand in marriage.

The varied tempo of the dialogue and the well-balanced contrasts deserve praise, but they are offset by the uneven aspect of the play's construction. And, though Marian appears to be the central figure, her two sisters steal the spotlight from her, especially in the bedroom scene of the second act, the first of its kind on the Abbey stage,[12] when they dominate the play as they conspire to encourage their father's wedding. The playwright is also inclined to insert random characters into farcical situations which show little or no reason for their existence other than to act as comic padding to cover the thinness of the plot. Notwithstanding these deficiencies, the play on its opening night received an extremely enthusiastic reception with many calls being made for the author. His absence in America at the time prevented this, so Dr. Walter Starkie on the Abbey Board of Directors had to deputize for him.[13]

III *Life in "Inish"*

Much as Trollope frequently returned to "Barchester" in his "Cathedral Stories," so Robinson in four of his last plays revisited Inish each time in fruitful exploration for sources of humor. He described it as "a small seaside town in Ireland, of not much importance save for the three summer months. . . . It has boarding houses but only one hotel of any size—The Seaview Hotel owned by Mr. John Twohig, who is the most important man in the town, chairman of most of the committees and a genial despot." In such wise Robinson prepared the way for a group of plays unified by having Inish or its rival seaside competitor, Shangarry Strand, as their locale.

The first and most successful of these which he himself directed was *Drama at Inish*,[14] later changed for production outside Ireland to *Is Life Worth Living?* He wrote it in a week while on vacation at a resort somewhat like Inish,[15] styling it *An Exaggeration in Three Acts*. In a curtain speech after the first night's performance, he explained why he had used such a different category for his play: "I wanted to confound the critics. It's really an absurd play based on an impossible situation. The critics would have described it as such, so you see I am saying it before them." [16]

The advice he gave himself in *Church Street*—to cling to the world he knew best for his writing sources—is now reiterated with a fresh slant; this time with much humor he indirectly satirizes his own cosmopolitan taste in drama. In a novel and shrewd mixing of simplicity with sophistication, he impishly insinuates that an overly intense taste for the joyless dramas of the Continental theatre, when foisted on a guileless and unprepared Irish countryside, can bring considerable unexpected unrest in its wake.

On the rather uproarious opening night on February 6, 1933, when even the actors laughed outright at some of the lines,[17] drama comes to Inish through the medium of the De la Mare Repertory Company, featuring two stagestruck, time-worn players, Hector de la Mare and his wife Constance Constantia. John Twohig, thinking that Inish is losing in the race for summer prestige and prosperity with the neighboring rival, Shangarry Strand, has invited them to provide the necessary uplift for the town.

As lovers of the ultra-serious side of the European theatre, the De la Mares delight in producing psychological and introspective dramas in the hope that they may revolutionize the souls of their audiences. Hector, always the actor, immediately upon his arrival assembles for himself a private audience in the hotel lounge composed of Twohig, his family, and his sister Lizzie to expound the aims of the repertory.

Hector   . . . I mean that some young man in the audience may see himself there on the stage, in all his lust, in all his selfishness, in all the cruelty of his youth, a young man such as your son. (He suddenly swings on Eddie, who shrinks away.)

Lizzie   Is it poor Eddie? There never was a more innocent boy.

Hector   I meant nothing personal. (And now it is John who inspires him.) Or some middle-aged man, in all outward appearances respectable, will see himself stripped naked, the sham cloak of virtue torn from his shoulders and he will stand exposed as the rotten sham he is. (And now it is Lizzie's and Annie's turn.) Women will see themselves vain, scheming for husbands, scheming for lovers.

Annie   Heaven defend us!

Lizzie   (awed)   'Tis like a mission.

Hector   It is a mission, Miss Twohig, a tremendous mission where the pulpit is the stage and great dramatists preach the sermons. I am myself a convert.

John   Do you mean you used to be a Protestant.

After ten days of this "mission," the mournful repertoire of the touring company makes quite an impression on the simple minds of the townspeople. But this imprint is a sinister one. The once peaceful community takes too literally and too much to heart the mood of these dramas: a general melancholy depresses the citizenry; suicides are quickly planned; wives suspect their husbands of infidelity; husbands begin to indulge in an extra drink or two for consolation; a politician even votes as he really thinks. Inish soon is the talk of Ireland.

At last Twohig deduces the cause of the trouble, and Inish is saved from a fate worse than death when, just in time, he replaces the De la Mare Repertory Company with a traveling circus.

The second of Robinson's "Inish" plays, *Bird's Nest,* presented for the first time at the Abbey on September 12, 1938, brings Robinson back to a theme used in *Harvest*—the evil doers of good. In a feebly and thinly woven plot, wherein the theme is frequently lost in unnecessary sidetracks—sidetracks that are meant to satirize Inish's lack of faith in itself—the play veers somewhat towards the tragic: a self-sacrificing father becomes an unwilling creator of evil.

Joseph Fehily, a worried and punctilious widower, tries hard to achieve a standard of genteel respectability for himself and his family. He centers all his hopes and dreams on the future success of his children. To arrive at this goal, he skimps and saves every penny he can; he constantly drives his children on to greater efforts in their studies. The more education they receive, the greater will be their accomplishments in the outside world. Inish will not have scope for the boundless horizons he envisions for them.

But the young ones, unknown to him, have dreams of their own. Hyacinth, the youngest, as an escape from the grinding studies at home, consoles himself with dreams of the day when he can be a ship radio operator roving the four seas. Josie, Fehily's only daughter and the pride of his heart, momentarily offers him fulfillment of his great expectations. She has been clever enough to win a fellowship to study music in Vienna, but she secretly wants a home of her own in Inish. Joseph's prospects are upset with the return of his brother-in-law to settle down in Inish after wandering around the world. The romance attached to his distant travels fascinates Hyacinth. Robinson at this point in his play is so engaged by this romantic mood that he inserts in his story a random character, Stan, chiefly as a vehicle for proclaiming his own preferred theme, the dreamer seeking contentment in his dreams:

Stan   My days are full. If it's a wet morning, I lie in bed reading till the sky clears; if it's a fine day, I'll be up with the sun walking the mountains, or down to the river throwing a line for a trout.

Joseph   And you call that a full day?

Stan   Oh, I'll be up half the night reading; and then there's the wireless. I spent a lot of money on a first class set and I have all Europe at my feet. . . .

Hyacinth   It sounds awful shut-in and lonely.

Stan   Not at all . . . if I want to talk I can walk two miles down to the village of an evening and have a few pints with the boys. But I don't go down once in a week except maybe to the school-house for the books from the county library—they've a great selection. I'm busy learning French and German, and now I can follow nearly everything they say on the wireless.

Joseph   It's shameful, shameful. A useless, idle life; a fine farm thrown away. What would become of the country if everyone carried on like that?

Stan   Sure they won't. The man who bought my land is plodding on it day and night. He's like a bit of the ground himself—clay and cowdung from boot to oxter. . . . He's happy and I'm happy and what else matters?

Soon this spirit of poetic protest against the humdrum brings the children's discontent to the surface: Hyacinth, aided by his aunt, runs away to sea; and Josie resolves to train the musical tastes of Inish rather than go to Vienna.

In an entertaining sidelight near the end of the play, the playwright introduces a brief sketch which allows him to make sly satirical thrusts at Irish foibles. He depicts two young clerks crossing paths, each looking forward to a more attractive life in the small town that the other is leaving.

Charlie   (He is as like Matt as possible; good looking, ordinary and well dressed.) Yes, it's a bit of luck for me coming East like this. Lord, I'm sick of the West.

Matt   I'm going there.

Charlie   God help you. . . .

Matt   Where are you staying?

Charlie   At the Seaview, just for a night or two till I find digs.

Matt   Good. We'll go over there and have a drink and you can tell me all about Westport.

Charlie   Right. I can give you a few tips and some intro's. —not that there's anyone worth knowing there. And you can give me the line on Inish.

Matt   There's no line on Inish. There's nothing to tell you.

Charlie   Why, it looks a darling little town.

Matt   Good Lord! Let's be going.

The play then winds to a close with the father's sacrifices coming to naught, and the last few moments disclose the disconsolate Joseph looking dejectedly out the window.

Robinson interrupted the "Inish" series with an innovation on Christmas Day, 1940, when Radio Eireann broadcast the first performance of his brief moral farce *Let Well Alone*. Following the pattern of Lady Gregory's *Spreading the News*, Robinson's radio playlet centers on the pranks of a young girl, Judy Roddy, who, by spreading false information about her seemingly lost sheep, desires to punish the local police for some imagined wrong they have inflicted on her. She pretends it is lost in a well; and, in trying to find the sheep, the police resurrect a collection of articles from the water better off left hidden there.

December 26, of the following year, witnessed Robinson's return to the "Inish" material in his next play, *Forget Me Not*. This time, though, he combined both Inish and Shangarry Strand for his setting. After the first night's performance at the Abbey, he made a curtain speech which indicated the purpose of his play: "I have written this play as a contradiction to a play, *Money Doesn't Matter*, which was played at this theatre some months ago." [18]

Forget Me Not somewhat reminds one of Pinero's *Thunderbolt* (1908); in the latter the families of four brothers are eager to divide a fortune among themselves and to leave the illegitimate daughter of the deceased without a share. The dead man was believed to have died intestate; but it is brought out later that the will, which one of the claimants purposefully destroyed, had really designated the illegitimate daughter as sole legatee of the money.

Robinson, in setting out to show that money does matter to the prospective beneficiaries of the O'Shea estate, begins unraveling the complexities of their relationship to establish the real heir. Until the unexpected arrival of Samuel Perrier from England, Fannie, a niece of the deceased, seems to have the best right to the property. Sam, alias Forget-Me-Not, turns out to be one of Robinson's unusual characters, notwithstanding the unevenness of the playwright's portraiture. Sam apparently ekes out a living in England peddling risqué French postcards under the guise of oriental goods; before that, he had tried with little success to sell vacuum cleaners.

When he arrives at the lawyer's office, Sam claims to be a grandnephew of the dead O'Shea. He is unable to prove this, since his traveling bag has been lost while coming to Shangarry Strand. The lawyers handling the case call Sam a fraud because of his odd history; but, fortunately for Sam, the bag is found and he joins the select group of candidates for the fortune.

Robinson revives his former interest in the non-realistic side of the drama by switching from his realistic manner to present in his second act the region of dreams and imagination. Fannie, at a birthday celebration in her honor, falls into a deep reverie about the past, and is carried back to the days of her grandparents, whom she imagines to be guiding her to a hidden drawer in her writing table.

When she awakens, she tests the reality of her dreams, only to find that the secret drawer conceals papers showing her to be an illegitimate child. For this reason she is no longer eligible for the O'Shea money. Sam is now left as the only legal heir. But the unpredictable Sam, when he discovers that the O'Shea fortune was earned by running gambling dens and by operating brothels in the United States, arranges to share the money with Fannie and the other claimants through the creation of the O'Shea Foundation. By this action he believes Fannie will be able to fulfill some of her ambitions for improving the community. In the very erratic and anti-climactic conclusion, Sam in tears leaves Shangarry Strand with the hope that he may return in the future. But after he departs, the vexatious money—now placed in the control of the members of the O'Shea Foundation—only causes renewed haggling.

During the academic year 1947-1948 Robinson returned to the United States for the last time. The previous year he had lectured at the University of North Carolina. While in New York on this last visit, he renewed earlier, cordial relations with Marc Connelly, who invited him to lecture to his playwriting class at the Yale School of Drama. This friendship continued until Robinson's death. As their countries' representatives in Oslo at the Fourth International Theatre Institute sponsored by UNESCO the two writers saw each other frequently and exchanged opinions about current movements in the American and European theatres. Their last meeting was in Dublin when Robinson was preparing with his coeditor Donagh MacDonagh to publish *The Oxford Book of Irish Verse* (1958). The two editors, Marc Connelly writes,[19] got into a hilarious and spirited argument with him over his complaints about the poets chosen and omitted, particularly over his criticism of their neglect of L. A. G. Strong.

During his last visit to the United States Robinson reworked the last of his "Inish" dramas, a three-act comedy entitled *The Lucky Finger*, which the Abbey had refused in the beginning of 1947. He also gave two seminars at Bowling Green University in Ohio during the fall semester at the invitation of Dean Emerson Shuck and Professor Elden T. Smith, now president of Ohio Wesleyan University. Commenting on Robinson's sojourn of six-months, Dean Shuck says, "He was exactly what we needed at the time. In some ways his coming to our campus marked a new era for the University, since he represented a widening of our horizons, which has continued steadily ever since." More specifically Dean Shuck admired Robinson's "gentle iconoclastic reaction to things about him," and his impatience "with stuffiness, protocol or hypocrisy."[20]

At Bowling Green, Robinson, under the encouraging eyes of his associates in the English and Speech departments, put the finishing touches to *The Lucky Finger*. Then on January 19, 1948, with the aid of his old Abbey friend, Sara Allgood, who came from Hollywood as guest player for the occasion, his play was performed at the University Theatre. After making some revisions in this version, Robinson again submitted it to the Abbey, which produced it on August 23 of the same year.

The standard of the playwright's craftsmanship in his last acted comedy of Irish life shows a falling off from his earlier high levels. He has recourse to some obvious theatrical tricks and devices, and his play subsides into a sentimental anticlimax at the finish.

Richard Clancy of Inish is a flourishing shopkeeper and a keen rival of John Twohig, the business leader of the town. Statia Clancy, his wife, acquires social aspirations to match her increasing financial importance. Through her, the playwright satirizes in a lightly humorous manner the social pretensions of the new middle classes in Ireland. Statia's sister-in-law, Julia—humble, middle aged, and dowdy, but a person with a heart of gold—is penniless and lives almost on sufferance with her brother Richard's family. Statia considers Julia as a stumbling block in her path towards social prominence in Inish; accordingly, she tries to shunt her off to another Clancy relative living on a farm in the hills outside the town. But Julia will not heed her sister-in-law; she likes Inish life too well for that.

An almost miraculous transformation suddenly occurs in the Clancy household when the meek and mild poor relation, Julia, wins a £500 award in a crossword puzzle competition. From that moment on, everything she does or touches brings her luck. Her simple charm endears her to an impoverished landlord, Sir Adrian Burke, who depends on his social prestige to provide a living for himself. Mrs. Clancy, to whom a titled person is a social power to be reckoned with, cannot, of course, imagine how Julia could attract any man, much less Sir Adrian.

Owing to her easily won wealth, Julia emerges as one of the outstanding people in Inish and as a magnet for all needing money to support their favorite causes. Because of her easygoing kindness, she is not long getting rid of her possessions; consequently, she believes that her luck has changed, that life will perhaps be very different in the future. Her fears, though, are momentarily allayed when she is informed that she has gained a £10,000 prize in the Irish Sweepstakes. But fortune's latest smile is only short lived, for she is told afterwards that this news was an error. Yet Sir Adrian does not heed this last reversal of hers; to him, her good luck still lies in herself and in her warm generous heart. The play concludes on a sentimentally optimistic note: Sir Adrian wins Julia's consent to marriage.

Recalling Robinson's unfulfilled expectations in his variegated pioneering plays, the wisdom of his decision to pursue again the call of the "Irish thing" cannot be gainsaid. It induced him to put to further use his admirable gifts as a genial, witty, detached interpreter of Irish life and failings. On the other hand, he apparently delayed too long his decision to return to the true font of his inspiration for it to exert its salutary powers upon his skills as a playwright. Thus his later plays about Irish life, even if frequently displaying his amiable satirical bent to good advantage, betray in their plot contrivances and in their theatricality a wearying of his creative energies. Perhaps if he had made up his mind to plumb more thoroughly the unexamined areas of the Irish scene earlier in his career when his creative fires were burning brightest, the upshot would have been more worthwhile not only for himself but also for the Irish theatre.

IV   *As the Curtain Falls*

In the last decade of Robinson's life, he received several honors as the grand old man of the Irish theatre and as the last link with its renowned past. After his return from the United States in 1948, Trinity College—the breeding ground for great Anglo-Irish dramatists ranging from Congreve to Beckett—bestowed on Robinson an honorary doctorate of literature for his contributions to Irish literature and the arts. He accepted his award with characteristic modesty. If people addressed him by his new title, he remarked that he did not like to be put into the same category as the Irish novelist, Edith Somerville, who, upon gaining a similar honorary degree, was quite irritated at those failing to call her "Doctor."

Robinson's dedicated zeal for the theatre made him prefer to die in harness, promoting the causes and ideals for which he had ceaselessly and tirelessly worked in the past without any material reward. Even when Robinson's "health was failing towards the last," writes Ernest Blythe, managing director of the Abbey, "and when he could not give as much attention as usual to scripts, he was asked to read one which was greatly overwritten and had scenes which contributed nothing to the impact of the play. Lennox, feeling pretty ill, wrote nothing on it except the words, 'A good play could be quarried out of this.' Ultimately the work was accorded the warmest reception. He had a keen scent for talent and I never knew him to condemn as worthless a script in which it was afterwards generally felt there was merit."[21]

It was typical also of Robinson that, during his remaining years, he should function as one of the pillars of the Actors' Church Union intended to assist theatrical people who had fallen on hard times. Much of the Union's success in its early days, recalls its chaplain, the Reverend George Hobson, could be attributed to Robinson's support: "His kindness was real and practical. As well as reaching into his own pocket, he would always appeal for maximum assistance for anyone seeking aid from the A. C. U. Benevolent Fund. He was kind hearted, generous to a fault. We who knew him well will always remember him as a very dear friend."[22]

In 1953, after recovering from an attack of angina suffered the preceding year, Robinson set out to foster the growth of amateur theatricals in Ireland. This was a goal very dear to him, since he sensibly believed that a truly national drama should be rooted in the people. A meeting of the Regional Festival Committees was called, and from it evolved the Amateur Drama Council of Ireland, which appointed Robinson its honorary patron and Brendan O'Brien, principal of Athlone Technical School, its organizing secretary.[23]

Robinson ranged far and wide throughout Ireland adjudicating at drama festivals. Truly, the amateur theatre became for him, W. Bridges Adams states, "something worth dying for. I believe he might be alive to this day, if he had not worn himself out in its service. Wherever this natural growth showed its head, there was Lennox fostering it, advising and above all inspiring; he brought magic into countless humdrum lives. As an adjudicator he could be scathing but he was always kind and gay. Towards the end there was little left of him but his spirit, but that was incandescent."[24]

Out of Robinson's experiences at these amateur competitions he, moreover, harvested the material for still another drama, *Speed the Plough*. This play deals humorously with the rise to fame of the rural village of Kilfinney when its dramatic club wins first prize at a provincial festival. This unpublished and unacted work, dedicated to the Young Farmers' Clubs in Ireland, Robinson designated as an *An Absurdity in Three Acts.*[25]

The year 1953 also saw Robinson make his second excursion into journalism as a contributor to the *Irish Press* of a weekly column of personal reminiscences, "I Sometimes Think." The best of these popular articles he subsequently selected and brought out as a book under the same title.

During the week of June 21, 1954, Hilton Edwards produced Robinson's last play, *The Demon Lover,* at the Gaiety Theatre. As a matter of fact, the script for this had been lying unfinished among Robinson's manuscripts since 1914. At that time, Yeats, aware of Robinson's study of Strindberg's plays, mentioned to him that perhaps the substance for a drama could be mined from the Swedish dramatist's half insane hatred of women.

Upon mulling over this suggestion, Robinson elicited like a genie from a bottle the idea of dramatizing the theme that evil minds have the power to compel others to do evil deeds. Since first acts came easily to Robinson, he soon got as far as writing the third act. But uncertainty about the prospects of his embryo drama being suitable for the Abbey's usual repertoire then crept in, so he did not finish the play.

Almost forty years later, the nearness of death impelled Robinson to complete his work, which he named after a quote from Coleridge's "Kubla Khan." The outcome was an unsuccessful, however valiant, attempt to cope with the difficult problem of characterizing genius in a convincing manner. Moreover, his dialogue is imprisoned in an out-of-date idiom more expressive of Dublin of at least a decade or more earlier.

Dominic Caughlan, "the demon lover" of the play, is a ruggedly handsome man in his fifties whose vibrant personality affects those under him. As a brilliant Irish entomologist and as a professor at a Dublin university, he has just been awarded the Nobel Prize for his outstanding publications about the habits of spiders and bees. His total absorption in the lower forms of life is to him a means of getting far away from the life of man. He is obsessed with the thought that, once he has made up his mind about a person's being bad, he must unfailingly be so.

Dominic has divorced his first wife and married Varina, a wealthy beauty, twenty years his junior. Varina's trust in Dominic is disturbed when his earnest young laboratory assistant, Roger Foley, talks about her husband's phobia. Before long, Dominic suspects her fidelity. One evening he arrives home unexpectedly from a banquet held in his honor and surprises her and Roger at their lovemaking. But Varina tells both men that she was merely pretending to be in love with Roger to unmask her husband. Having found out the truth about him, she departs "laughing at two silly very, very clever men." [26]

In 1956, Robinson had a second heart attack; but, while recuperating at the Bon Secour Hospital in Cork, his indomitable nature would not let him idle. Some of his undertakings he mentions in correspondence from there, dated May 18, 1956, to the present writer: "I believe the last attack was touch and go and the next one will be definitely *go*. I have been making long-playing disks of Yeats's poems and one side of reminiscences. There is another to be done and that frets me. It's for the U.S.A. I also actually did a quarter of an hour recording for the B.B.C. in honour of Somerville and Ross's forthcoming hundreth birthday. The doc gingered me up and I did it from the bed and no one would think I was ill at all. Silly old man will he ever stop!"[27]

A month after Robinson left the hospital, the Communist Chinese government, through an agent, officially invited him as the senior Irish dramatist to lecture at the centenary celebrations for Shaw's birthday in Peking. He was joined by Gerda Ring, Director of the National Theatre of Oslo, who represented Norway at the companion ceremonies for the fiftieth anniversary of Ibsen's death. Since the nuances of politics meant little to Robinson, he did not see anything wrong in accepting this offer. But, on the day he left for China, the *Irish Press* without any warning—and much to Robinson's surprise and regret—stopped his articles.

When he came back to Dublin in August after traveling for four weeks in different Chinese cities, he penned a series of three articles, "Through the Bamboo Curtain," for the *Irish Times* about his observations of the Chinese theatre and the Shaw-Ibsen ceremonies.[28] He particularly noted that Shaw's *Mrs. Warren's Profession* and Ibsen's *A Doll's House* were the most popular plays of these writers with Chinese audiences. Wondering why, he found out they were highly regarded because they dramatized a vital subject in contemporary Communist China: the emancipation of women.

Lady Longford, Director of the Dublin Gate Theatre, who with her late husband was a long time friend of Robinson, remembers her last meeting with him a few days before his death in 1958: "Lennox against doctor's orders was working hard at a Church Union Sale of Work. He was, as ever, tireless in raising funds, he was always good at that, a persistent beggar for charity. . . . I met him soon after I came to Ireland in 1925, and the amazing thing is that he never changed in appearance from then until he died; he seemed to grow no older." [29] Robinson was buried in St. Patrick's Cathedral in Dublin not far from the tombs of Dean Swift and Stella, his partner in one of the most enigmatic of love affairs in literary annals; it was a mark of esteem that would never have entered Robinson's mind.

CHAPTER 7

Versatile Craftsman and
Man of the Theatre

IRISH history during the present century recorded notable and influential changes in the political, social, and economic aspects of Irish life. Irish writers effectively mirrored these variations. From the earliest days of the renaissance of Irish letters until about 1922, the Irish author generally colored Irish life with fanciful hues, giving his fellow countrymen and peoples of other lands a picture of a poetic and romantic race. Even the realism of the early "peasant" dramas held, as Sean O'Faolain observed, "the charm of external novelty—dress, speech, situation, humor." [1]

Two events completely altered this nostalgic outlook: the catharsis effected on the Irish mind as a result of the rebellion of 1916, and the disillusionment created in the Irish spirit as an aftermath of the Civil War. Although witnesses of a terrible beauty born, the people had been told that their dreams of centuries were with O'Leary in the grave. The new Ireland, relatively free from English political control through the Anglo-Irish treaty, began to work towards improving its own social and economic conditions. The subsequent strengthening of Irish industry and commerce brought into prominence the growing importance, prestige, and self-satisfaction of the middle classes.

Both novelists and playwrights quickly responded to these fundamental transformations in the pattern of Irish history. Some of the commonest sources of inspiration for the earlier realistic literature of the Irish literary revival centered on wills, mortgages, and marriage contracts; these subjects were used to the point of abuse. Later the young playwrights or novelists came to regard these topics as old fashioned. Instead, with a fresh awareness and more critical eyes, they scrutinized the newer experiences at their disposal: the drift away from the country to the towns and cities, and the increased sophistication of a recently freed people. True, the dialect dramas of rural life were not completely forgotten; in fact, they still remained the nucleus of the Abbey repertoire. But the verve and the exploratory mood of the more modern school of playwrights carried them beyond the limits of the traditional "Abbey" play into an ever-widening range of literary investigation. To avoid the restrictions of the established pattern, notably the simplicity of the earlier plays, these playwrights moved in the more cosmopolitan theatrical circles of experimentation and expressionism.

Robinson's plays offer an unusually good and reliable source for observing these new and multifarious forces in evolution in Ireland. Before his death, he ranked as the "senior dramatist" of the Abbey with almost fifty fruitful years as a writer for the stage behind him. He vied with Lady Gregory as being the most prolific of all the Irish dramatists of the twentieth century, but he was more versatile than she. His versatility, indeed, constitutes one of his striking points. For none of his plays repeat themselves: his fund of knowledge of life and society is too broad, his watch on their changes too intent to permit that. In such wise over the years he contributed greatly to the needs of the Abbey repertoire for interesting, entertaining plays.

From his earliest days as a playwright, Robinson was always in the vanguard of original trends in the Irish theatre. While searching for different styles and for other directions in the theatre, he acquired a sophistication of style in viewing his material equaled by very few Irish writers. A rapid glance at the scope of his plays indicates the broadness of his interests. From his first realistic and "problem" plays about the countryman and the small-town shopkeeper, he turned to political dramas, fantasy, satirical comedies, comedies of manners, farce, psychological dramas, expressionistic and experimental plays.

Though close to the poetic and romantic idealism of Yeats and his colleagues in the Irish Literary Renaissance, the deeper instincts of Robinson's nature were far more responsive to the objective study of Irish life already taking shape in the hands of such dramatists as Lady Gregory, Boyle, and Colum. Thus he was following the general tendency of that time. The realistic spirit was in the air and life was an earnest matter, full of problems for the artist and thinker to analyze or solve. In the theatre the impact of such dramatists as Ibsen, Shaw, Barker, and Galsworthy was making itself felt on the aims of most of the younger playwrights, including the Irish.

Reflecting this serious purposiveness concerning world affairs, Robinson hoped his earlier dramas, particularly his "thesis" plays, would help his generation in Ireland to make an effective, faithful appraisal of themselves and of their social and political problems. "We must," he said, "criticize ourselves ruthlessly." If this were done, the frequently sentimental estimate held in the past about Ireland might be corrected; and the new Ireland, no longer oversensitive to criticism, but conscious of its revived strength, would be able to rectify its flaws and to build again on more reliable foundations.

To the realism of Synge and Colum, Robinson added a harshly ironic note. And in his careful observation and simple natural reporting of the tumult of the passing parade of events he deadened the unique poetic strains characterizing the realism of his predecessors. The plays of Robinson's earlier period helped to unfold a long series of similar works. Thus realism evolved as a force in the Irish theatre; and, at the same time, a barricade was erected against Yeats's aspirations for the growth of poetic drama in Ireland.

But behind Robinson's realism lingers a strain of romanticism that had its effects upon his subconscious all during his career as a playwright. His nearness to the inspiring idealism of the founders of the Irish Literary Renaissance and the influence of Yeats upon him—always a very important element in Robinson's life—to a great extent explain the origins of his fondness for the hidden quixotic aspects of life's struggles. One is introduced to it briefly in the thwarted aspirations of Ellen in *The Cross Roads* and in the disillusioned dreaming of Mary in *Harvest*. Later it ripened in his three political plays—*Patriots, The Dreamers,* and *The Lost Leader*—in which he images Yeats's somewhat utopian outlook on the Irish political scene. Here one notices very clearly what is in all probability Robinson's favorite theme: the dreamer and idealist attempting to cope with the realities of existence. He echoes it again and again throughout his subsequent plays, either loudly or softly as the material at his disposal demands. Sometimes these echoes are found without any cause for their existence as in *Bird's Nest,* where his fondness for romanticism weakens the structure of his play. Unfortunately, judging from the indulgent atmosphere of two of his last plays, *Forget Me Not* and *The Lucky Finger,* his underlying romantic streak had softened into an easy sentimentalism. In them he accepted without reservation what once he would have trenchantly criticized.

His dreamers respond to the complexities and ironies of reality in different ways. On one hand, like Daisy in *The Round Table,* they may find the constant dull routine of daily life too monotonous and try to escape into a land of dreams; or, like Peter in *Portrait,* they may find that they are bereft of secure ties or values, and, when they see that the burdens before them are intolerable, they quit life. Or, as the author's counterbalance, they may accept the tragedy of defeat, as James Nugent does in *Patriots;* or they may wish to carry on the fight for their dreams, as Kate does in *The Big House* or as Will does in *The White Blackbird.* Through these characters, Robinson tried to exemplify his belief: "Dreams are the only permanent things in life."

One can more clearly observe Robinson becoming a leader of trends in the Irish theatre in 1913, when he was producer at the Abbey. In that year he attempted to supply the need for diversity at the Abbey by familiarizing the Irish public with the life of European countries as seen through the eyes of such dramatists as Strindberg and Hauptmann. Five years later through the Drama League—this time more forcefully—he also sought to bring fresh models from the European and American theatres to the attention of Irish writers. He hoped thereby to help them extend their literary perspectives beyond the provincial confines of the "Abbey" play. His own writing began to show the influx of his cosmopolitan interests. And for a span of twelve years between 1922 and 1934, which he devoted mainly to experimenting and extending the range of his dramatic vision, his plays with few exceptions are non-Irish in setting.

But this projection of himself beyond the Irish scene into realms about which he knew comparatively little and his uncertainty about the manner in which he might successfully accomplish his objectives led to his failure. This he conceded in

1934 in his partly autobiographical play, *Church Street.* Therein he told his audience that it is only helpful for the Irish writer to imitate the example of other nations in so far as their techniques can be applied to the Irish society he knows best; that the "Irish thing" in his life must be given primary attention, must be deemed the true fountainhead of his art. It would seem, however, that he arrived too late at this significant decision regarding his approach to playwriting. Even though he attempted to follow his own advice for effecting the best results in his creative work, a waning of his once superior powers as a theatrical craftsman became evident in the plays that follow *Church Street.*

Robinson's many-sided pioneering efforts affected the writing of his Abbey contemporaries. Brinsley MacNamara, who in 1919 infused the Abbey with his fresh and needed talents, praised Robinson as a leader in new tendencies in the Irish drama and as a cosmopolitan guide for the younger playwrights.[2] T. C. Murray, too, when lecturing at the Abbey Theatre Festival in 1938, at which Yeats made his last public appearance, acknowledged the special appeal Robinson's early plays had had for him as a young writer. In the rural folk of the writings of Yeats, Synge, and Lady Gregory there was no similarity to the country people of his native county, Cork, whom he knew intimately. To him the works of these authors appeared to be charming adventures in make-believe. But what he observed in Robinson's dramas struck close to home, for Robinson showed him that "in the very traffic of every day life from which we turned our eyes, there was potential comedy and tragedy. . . . In their way of thought, their speech, their accent, the people that he created were the people I knew. From the field, the farmhouse, the shop, the wayside tavern, they seemed to have wandered on to his stage."[3]

At first glance, the plays of Teresa Deevy would not appear to indicate any indebtedness to Robinson, for she is much less concerned with establishing the realities of background and setting. She prefers instead to look with subtle and sensitive vision into the minds of introspective young women romantically seeking refuge in their imaginations from their humdrum and even harsh existence. Here then in this spirit of romantic escapism lie the kindred ties of the two playwrights.

Robinson's comments explain the beginnings of what grew into a close friendship between the two writers: "I sent Miss Deevy a book of my half-realistic plays and I know she was affected by them and started to make her own half-realistic plays but all of them so much better than my own."[4] Miss Deevy admired Robinson's dramas, she said, "because there was a 'wonderment' about them. Lennox never lost this gift of childhood, although he could mock when in another mood." Writing further about her associations with Robinson in the 1930's, she went on to tell about his guidance: "Once when I had not brought out my meaning clearly enough, he smilingly told me, 'Remember that everything must be said three times, once for the intelligent audience, twice for the unintelligent and the third for the critics.' "[5]

Yet Robinson tried to be careful of how much advice he offered, making plain why he did so: "I destroyed many plays long ago by thinking when I read them for Abbey production I could get the author to rewrite them or make my suggested changes. The result was always very disappointing—I had spoiled their own special touch."[6]

Robinson, too, did much to encourage George Shiels, one of the most popular and prolific of the Abbey writers. The appeal of his broad humor to the general public in search of entertainment made money for the Abbey. As a matter of fact, the comic spirit of the two authors acted as a fittingly timed tonic for the Irish people, giving them joy and the gift of laughing at themselves. While an aspiring playwright without any knowledge of his craft, Shiels was attracted to Robinson's satirical works; thus, for example, in the most popular of Shiels's comedies, *The New Gossoon*, in 1930, he has conscious memories of Robinson's *The Whiteheaded Boy*. In both plays there is the same good nature; the same modern and gay young man gains maturity through rejecting parental restraints.

Robinson's principal asset lies in his all-round, thorough experience of the theatre. Certainly, his lengthy record of devoted service to the Abbey as writer, producer, actor, manager, director, and general troubleshooter made him a pillar of strength for that theatre, and hence deserving of the title, Ireland's "man of the theatre."

With the death of Lady Gregory in 1932, the previously active

Abbey Theatre showed signs of decline. An aging Yeats had gradually lost interest in guiding the national theatre. Robinson, without the firm support of Lady Gregory, was this time not equal to the task of rejuvenating the Abbey, notwithstanding his past, successful heroic efforts. For the remaining years of his life he was faced with recurring sharp criticism about the policies of the Abbey directorate and about deteriorating Abbey standards. No one—writers, actors, audiences—escaped censure. Robinson, nevertheless, as a playwright, remained hopeful until his death that the Abbey would again win international renown through the pens of its dramatists, that some new genius would erupt to equal Synge and O'Casey. Even when it was burned in 1951, he took comfort in the fact that the modern theatre replacing it, through its component parts, would be the future home not only for the traditional "Abbey" plays but also for the plays of America, of Europe, and of Gaelic-speaking Ireland.

Having directed at the Abbey for almost as long as he had been a playwright, he knew intimately the needs of the actor. And his highly developed theatre sense gives his plays more polish and makes his structure better shaped than those of any of his Irish contemporaries. His expert technique as a craftsman in the theatre comes to light in the manner in which he builds up his succinct and frequently underwritten lines so that they acquire enough strength for an affecting artistic whole. His ability in giving vitality and interest to the light conversational interplay of his characters frequently carries what appears at the outset to be the merest trivia of dialogue—inadequate for a satisfactory play—into a dramatic first- or second-act curtain.

In his use of language Robinson is far removed from the poetic exuberance of Synge's imaginative world. Whatever similarity exists between the two writers would seem to stem from their shared somber cast of mind. The simple and even terse directness of Robinson's lines is more like the English naturalists to whom he is indebted for his early practical experiences in the theatre. His dialogue in this respect suggests an eavesdropper on the uneven flow of talk used in the daily activities of life.

Robinson does not have Colum's penetration into the workings of the Irish mind. This said, one is compelled to add that—considering his upbringing in the staunchly Unionist, conservative, and Protestant circles of his family—it is all the more remarkable to find how much perceptive understanding he has of the hearts and minds of those in the Irish scene beyond the rectory walls of his father's home: the environment of the farmer, the shopkeeper, the townsman. Furthermore, he scrutinizes Irish society without any of the self-conscious mannerisms of earlier Anglo-Irish writers, who generally viewed the Irish as a humorous and quaint people, full of exotic appeal for English readers.

Except in such plays of Robinson's novice days as *Harvest* and *The Cross Roads,* through which he hoped to propagate his personal theories about Irish life, he is fundamentally objective and devoid of argument. Moreover, his quite dexterous handling of his material suggests a skillful observer able to probe thoroughly into the hearts of those characters winning his attention.

Yet, at the same time, he manages to keep a certain aloofness, to retain an esthetic distance, which does not allow him to show too much concern with the final lot of his characters. He prefers, much like Chekhov, to stand on a remote observation pedestal and in this way avoid becoming involved in the main current of events ebbing and flowing about him. Probably the best example of this characteristic is found in one of his finest plays, *The Big House.* With an air of good-mannered tolerance he admirably attempts to portray a balanced picture of the turbulent Irish political scene as it influenced the Anglo-Irish landlord class. By adopting this attitude of detachment Robinson contrasts sharply with Sean O'Casey, who frequently envelopes himself emotionally in his characters.

No doubt Robinson's dramas, as Camillo Pellizzi, the Italian historian of the theatre pointed out, played a part in calling the attention of American playwrights in the early decades of this century to the unique and vital dramatic resources at their doorsteps.[7] But more important for Robinson's international standing is the judgment of English, American, Swiss, and French critics—among them William Archer, Allardyce Nicoll, George Jean Nathan, John Gassner, Kaspar Spinner, and Anatole Rivoallan[8]—all of whom praise Robinson's ability as a writer of comedy. Because of their favorable consensus, Robinson is best known today throughout the international theatre as a gay, sympathetic observer and critic of the imperfections of the Irish people in his comedies of Irish family life; in fine, he is a modern

Goldsmith. His comedies also hold within them his future reputation as a playwright. To date, few contemporary comedies in the English language have retained their popularity with audiences as long as Robinson's two outstanding successes, *The Whiteheaded Boy* and *The Far-Off Hills*.[9]

Hence it can be seen that Robinson has his share of the chief attributes needed to make an outstanding dramatist. For all that, he also has certain deficiencies that hinder him from achieving that rank. One of the first of these noticeable weaknesses in quite a few of his dramas is the thinness of his plots. His versatility and his too-rapid writing create the impression of facility but not of thoroughness. Besides, whenever his imagination fails him, he falls back on the wide technical knowledge of the theatre at his command to aid him in filling out his play to desired proportions. This tendency is most evident in his flair for introducing in his plays intensely melodramatic scenes illustrative more of the sphere of the theatre rather than of actuality.

There is still another, even greater defect perceivable in nearly all his plays, especially his serious ones. In advancing the destiny of his characters to their ultimate goal, he leaves behind a tantalizing, dissatisfied impression that some element or quality is missing. This effect is all the more disappointing because most of his plays begin in an engaging manner; he is remarkably deft at arousing interest by effective use of contrasts and suspense, considerably accomplished in the construction of his first acts. But at the end of his play, one is left somewhat puzzled at the loose ends that such an experienced craftsman has left untied behind him.

The chief cause for this weakness would seem to rest in his failure to arrive at a unity of impression or purpose based on some integrating principle or view of the universe for interpreting the flow of daily events. In the absence of any underlying philosophy of life—his true innerself always retains silence—he does not involve himself in treating the fundamental problems of good and evil; such matters as conscience and morality are not foremost in his plays.[10] Robinson's concerns, in spite of his serious and even tragic sense of the human condition, apparently lie principally with the transient, topical affairs of daily living, and on this account he is prevented from being classed with the great dramatists. He is rather, at his best, an excellent theatrical craftsman, who well merits a place among the most entertaining and versatile of his kind in the English-speaking theatre of modern times.

Notes and References

Preface
1. Correspondence from Denis Johnston to Michael J. O'Neill.

Chapter One
1. "Lennox Robinson," *University Review*, II: No. 5, 59.
2. A taped interview with Hilton Edwards.
3. Lennox Robinson, *Curtain Up* (London, 1942), p. 12.
4. Lennox Robinson, *Three Homes* (London, 1938), p. 49.
5. *Ibid.*, p. 51.
6. *Ibid.*, pp. 129-30.
7. *Ibid.*, p. 154.
8. *Ibid.*, p. 71. Robinson also noted, "I have always been attracted by elderly spinsters."
9. *Ibid.*, p. 131.
10. *Ibid.*, p. 155. See also p. 128, where he says, "I think my parents gave me a very bad book education—not altogether their fault—but they gave me a wise education morally."
11. *Ibid.*, pp. 176-77.
12. *Ibid.*, p. 174.
13. Lennox Robinson, "In the Days of My Youth," *T.P's and Cassell's Weekly*, February 6, 1926.
14. *Loc. cit.*
15. *Curtain Up*, p. 15.
16. *Three Homes*, p. 180.

Chapter Two
1. *The Irish Dramatic Movement*, 2nd ed. (London, 1939), p. xiii.
2. For the history of the Fay brothers confer W. G. Fay and Catherine Carswell, *The Fays of the Abbey Theatre*, London, 1935.
3. See Robinson's *Pictures in a Theatre* (Dublin, 1947), p. 8, where he regards Colum's kind of realism as the bridge between his own realistic mode and the original poetic-heroic theatre.
4. Lennox Robinson "Twenty Years Ago," *The Irish Statesman*, October 8, 1927.

5. *Loc. cit.*

6. "This Set Me Thinking," an unpublished manuscript among Robinson's private papers.

7. *Three Homes*, p. 218.

8. *Curtain Up*, pp. 18-19.

9. *Loc. cit.*

10. "This Set Me Thinking."

11. Lady Gregory, *Our Irish Theatre* (New York, 1914), p. 99.

12. October 9, 1908.

13. *The Abbey Theatre and Irish Plays* (The Irish National Theatre Movement in Three Year's Work at the Abbey Theatre Told in Press Cuttings), II, 86. William A. Henderson gave his four volume collection of cuttings, letters, and notes to the National Library of Ireland.

14. October 17, 1908.

15. *Three Homes*, p. 222.

16. *Loc. cit.*

17. Henderson, IV, 118.

18. J. M. Kerrigan, one of the other leading actors in the company, expressed, however, the hope that, when the play would be given at Cork, the audience would show its resentment.

19. *Curtain Up*, pp. 21-22.

20. *Dramatis Personae* (London, 1936), pp. 131-32.

21. Correspondence from Daniel Corkery to Michael J. O'Neill.

22. *Three Homes*, p. 224.

23. Correspondence from Rutherford Mayne to Michael J. O'Neill.

24. *Three Homes*, p. 225.

25. Quoted with the permission of the Society of Authors and the Public Trustee. Among Robinson's papers are this letter and Shaw's wire to Lady Gregory, "I begin rehearsing a new play Monday for production on 23. Feb. Could take Robinson as hon. sec. for that if he were in London."

26. Archibald Henderson, *George Bernard Shaw: Man of the Century* (New York, 1956), p. 674.

27. *Curtain Up*, pp. 26-27.

28. *Ibid.*, p. 31.

29. See the entry for May 19, 1910 in Joseph Holloway's diaries, *The Impressions of a Dublin Playgoer (1899-1944)*. Noted in Dublin as an avid theatregoer and first nighter, Holloway willed his voluminous collection of theatrical memoirs to the National Library of Ireland.

30. *Curtain Up*, p. 33.

31. *Ibid.*, p. 22.

32. Quoted from Holloway's diary volume for June-December 1910, p. 746.

Chapter Three

1. Quoted from Lennox Robinson's *Ireland's Abbey Theatre* (London, 1951), p. 86.
2. *Curtain Up,* p. 32.
3. Quoted from Robinson's incompleted manuscript on the life of Lady Gregory, p. 31.
4. *Ibid.* See also Lady Gregory's *Our Irish Theatre,* Chapter 4, which discusses the rioting over *The Playboy* in America. In his incompleted life of Lady Gregory, Robinson mentions that when Thomas Hardy watched the Abbey Company act this play in London, he appeared rather puzzled by it.
5. *The Splendid Years* (Dublin, 1955), p. 132.
6. *Curtain Up,* p. 44.
7. *Ibid.,* p. 44. Several months after the first production of *Patriots* George Pierce Baker, then seeking ideas for the stage of the Agassiz House Auditorium at Harvard, visited Robinson at the Abbey to learn about Gordon Craig's devises in use there. While in Dublin, Baker saw *Patriots;* and though he did not like the curtain on act one, he judged the play to be "well characterized, a moving simple play of great promise for Robinson's future. It lifts him out of the experimental stage." Cf. W. P. Kinne, *George Pierce Baker and the American Theatre* (Cambridge, Mass., 1954), pp. 164-65.
8. Holloway, January 21, 1919.
9. Letter from Geraldine Cummins to Michael J. O'Neill.
10. Lennox Robinson, "Yeats, the Man and the Dramatist," *Scattering Branches,* ed. Stephen Gwynn (New York, 1940), p. 78.
11. Letter from Dr. Walter Starkie to Michael J. O'Neill.
12. Letter from Dr. Monk Gibbon to Michael J. O'Neill.
13. Taped interview with Hilton Edwards.
14. Correspondence from Shelah Richards to Michael J. O'Neill.
15. Correspondence from Teresa Deevy to Michael J. O'Neill.
16. "Problem Plays," *The Irish Theatre,* ed. Lennox Robinson (London, 1939), pp. 217-18.
17. *Curtain Up,* p. 221.
18. *The History of the American Theatre* (New York, 1951), p. 369.
19. *Curtain Up,* pp. 74-75.
20. Yeats, too, had said, "I go back to Calderon. Not only things but dreams themselves are a dream."
21. In his treatment of history, Robinson claimed that his object was to deal with it realistically and not to gloss over the cowardice and treachery that led to Emmet's defeat nor to omit noting the failing in Emmet's character. "I was," he explained, "only copying the

headlines Lady Gregory set in her Folk-History Plays." See his *Pictures in a Theatre*, p. 21.

22. Holloway, July 28, 1923.

23. *Curtain Up*, p. 79.

24. Extract from letter quoted in *Curtain Up*, p. 89.

25. *Dark Days* (Dublin, 1918), p. 15.

26. Holloway, February 19, 1918.

27. *The Old Drama and the New* (London, 1923), p. 370.

28. This excerpt is from a letter sent from Grove Lodge, Hampstead, July 13, 1919. Robinson included it in a special scrapbook for personal memorabilia, which he collected for a while early in his career at his mother's suggestion.

29. Yeats's note is among the items in Robinson's scrapbook.

30. Moore's letter also is in Robinson's scrapbook.

31. See the preface to *The Lost Leader*.

Chapter Four

1. *Curtain Up*, p. 106. Archer in *The Old Drama and the New*, p. 370, rated *The Whiteheaded Boy* without peer as a peasant comedy. In London it ran for 290 performances during 1920 and 1921 at the Ambassador Theatre, thus it broke all records for length of run of an Irish play in England.

2. Letter from Mrs. Ganly to Michael J. O'Neill. Confer *Palette and Plough*, Dublin, 1948, for further details about his life with the O'Briens at Cahirmoyle.

3. Quoted from a letter in *Curtain Up*, p. 110.

4. Quoted from Yeats's letter to Lady Gregory in Joseph Hone's *W. B. Yeats* (New York, 1943), pp. 341-42.

5. *Lady Gregory's Journals*, ed. Lennox Robinson (London, 1946), p. 55.

6. *Ibid.*, p. 61.

7. *Loc. cit.*

8. Letter from Elizabeth Coxhead to Michael J. O'Neill.

9. Both letters were published in the Dublin *Evening Telegraph*, November 22, 1919.

10. Quoted from his incompleted life of Lady Gregory.

11. *Lady Gregory's Journals*, pp. 173-74.

12. *Curtain Up*, p. 131. See also *Lady Gregory's Journals*, pp. 70-71, for Robinson's letter to Lady Gregory explaining what happened when he decided to keep the Abbey open during the Civil War.

13. *Curtain Up*, p. 138. See p. 139 for O'Casey's letter of thanks to Robinson and Lady Gregory for their consideration in reading his difficult ms.

14. Holloway, March 18, 1924.

15. Sean O'Casey, *Inisfallen Fare Thee Well* (New York, 1949), p. 235.

16. Correspondence from Sean O'Casey to Michael J. O'Neill.

17. Tyrone Guthrie, *A Life in the Theatre* (New York, 1959), p. 294.

18. *The Observer*, August 2, 1925.

19. *Curtain Up*, p. 135.

20. *Lady Gregory's Journals*, p. 277. See also pp. 278-79.

21. *Curtain Up*, p. 135. See also *Lady Gregory's Journals*, pp. 280-282. In his letter to her, p. 282, he charged that his dismissal was a victory for the obscurantists.

22. *Curtain Up*, p. 132.

23. *The Contemporary Theatre, 1925* (London, 1926), p. 119.

24. *Curtain Up*, p. 106.

25. Correspondence from Norris Davidson to Michael J. O'Neill.

26. The Library of Congress holds a copy of the manuscript of the play under its original title, *The Revolt of the Swans.*

Chapter Five

1. Mrs. Iris Wise allowed me to make a transcript of Robinson's letter to her father, James Stephens.

2. Quoted from the *Dublin Drama League Collected Programmes* (*1914-1936*), in National Library of Ireland.

3. Correspondence from Denis Johnston to Michael J. O'Neill.

4. *Curtain Up*, pp. 119-20.

5. Holloway, April 27, 1924.

6. *Ibid.*, November 29, 1925.

7. *Curtain Up*, p. 220.

8. See *Lady Gregory's Journals*, p. 102, where she commends Robinson's "Spanish taste."

9. *Lady Gregory's Journals*, p. 107.

10. *Ibid.*, p. 92.

11. Holloway, October 13, 1925.

12. Quoted from the incompleted life of Lady Gregory.

13. *Ibid.*

14. Correspondence from Professor Merriam to Michael J. O'Neill.

15. *Curtain Up*, p. 151.

16. *Ibid.*, p. 153.

17. Quoted from Arthur and Barbara Gelb's *O'Neill* (New York, 1955), p. 770.

18. Quoted from *The Letters of W. B. Yeats*, ed. Alan Wade (New York, 1955), p. 770.

19. Professor Canfield allowed me to read and transcribe Robinson's letter to him.

20. "This Set me Thinking."

21. The program for this play is among the bound collected programs for 1931 in the archives of the Abbey Theatre.

22. Interview with Hilton Edwards.

23. *Loc. cit.*

24. Correspondence from Shelah Richards to Michael J. O'Neill.

25. Miss Deevy placed at my disposal Robinson's letters to her.

Chapter Six

1. *Curtain Up*, p. 224.

2. *Synge and Anglo-Irish Literature* (Cork, 1947), p. 9.

3. *In Wicklow, West Kerry, The Congested Districts, Under Ether* (Boston, 1912), p. 45.

4. See Robinson's *Bryan Cooper* (London, 1941), pp. 43-45.

5. *Curtain Up*, p. 98.

6. *Bryan Cooper*, pp. 88-89.

7. *Curtain Up*, p. 98.

8. Quoted from Hone, p. 371.

9. The play was not published. The typescript forms part of Robinson's private papers.

10. Holloway, August 18, 1936.

11. *Four Plays of Serafín and Joaquín Alvarez Quintero*, trans. Helen and Harley Granville-Barker, London, 1927. *The Women Have Their Way*, was produced at the Abbey a month after *The Far-Off Hills*.

12. Holloway notes that Robinson has several such precedents to his name at the Abbey, including an abortion scene in *Church Street* and the first use of the word "bloody."

13. Holloway, October 22, 1928.

14. The success of this play in London encouraged Robinson to direct a production of it in New York. But it closed on Broadway after a brief run there. See *Curtain Up*, pp. 159-60. After *The Far-Off Hills*, *Drama at Inish* ranks as the third most popular of his plays. Following these in order of success come *Crabbed Youth and Age, The Lost Leader*, and *The Big House*.

15. In *Curtain Up*, p. 106, Robinson comments on his rapid writing: "When I write, I write very rapidly and boast of writing *Drama at Inish* in a week and *The Far-Off Hills* in three, but the idea behind them lies dormant for months."

16. *Irish Press*, February 7, 1933.

17. Holloway, February 6, 1933.

18. *Irish Times*, December 27, 1941.

19. Correspondence from Marc Connelly to Michael J. O'Neill.

20. Correspondence from Dean Emerson Shuck to Michael J. O'Neill.

21. Correspondence from Ernest Blythe to Michael J. O'Neill.

22. Correspondence from the Reverend George Hobson to Michael J. O'Neill.

23. See the *Irish Times,* May 12, 1962, for an interview with Brendan O'Brien which gives the background of the evolution of the amateur drama movement in Ireland.

24. Correspondence from W. Bridges-Adams to Michael J. O'Neill.

25. Shortly before he died, the playwright sent me the script of *Speed the Plough.*

26. Mrs. Lennox Robinson made available to me the scripts for *The Demon Lover* and for the unacted adaption of Turgenev's *Fathers and Sons.*

27. Correspondence from Lennox Robinson to Michael J. O'Neill.

28. See the *Irish Times* for September 3, 4, and 5, 1956.

29. Letter from Lady Longford to Michael J. O'Neill.

Chapter Seven

1. *The Irish* (West Drayton, Middlesex, 1947), p. 137.

2. *Abbey Plays: 1899-1948* (Dublin, 1949), p. 17.

3. "George Shiels, Brinsley MacNamara, etc.," *The Irish Theatre,* p. 124.

4. Quoted from Robinson's review of her *Three Plays,* London, 1939 in *The Dublin Magazine,* XV (April-June), 71-72.

5. Correspondence from Teresa Deevy to Michael J. O'Neill.

6. Quoted from Robinson's letter to Teresa Deevy.

7. *The English Drama,* trans. Rowan Williams (London, 1935), p. 221.

8. Cf. the following: Archer's *The Old Drama and the New;* Nicoll's *British Drama; The Intimate Notebooks of George Jean Nathan;* Gassner's *Masters of Drama;* Spinner's *Die Alte Dame Sagt: Nein!;* Rivoallan's *Littérature Irlandaise Contemporaine.* See also Shotaro Oshima, *A Study of Modern Irish Literature,* Tokyo, 1960.

9. Translation of these plays have been made into various languages including Welsh and Gaelic. During his lifetime one of Robinson's favorite exhibits to his friends was a Hungarian translation of *The Far-Off Hills.*

10. Gerald Heard, noted mystical philosopher who as secretary for Sir Horace Plunkett was a friend of Robinson, writes me, "Lennox did not enter into philosophic argument; he was alien to philosophic thought."

Selected Bibliography

PRIMARY SOURCES

See the Chronology in this volume for information about Robinson's published works. It also includes the dates of the first productions of his plays at the Abbey and at other theatres and indicates which of his own plays he directed while producer at the Abbey. Consult his history, *Ireland's Abbey Theatre*, London: Sidgwick and Jackson, Ltd., 1951, for a list of all the plays he directed there and their casts.

SECONDARY SOURCES

Agate, James. *The Contemporary Theatre, 1925.* London: Chapman and Hall, Ltd., 1926. See pp. 119-20 for an entertaining and perceptive review of *The Round Table.*

Archer, William. *The Old Drama and the New,* Boston: Small, Maynard and Co., 1923. He praises highly *The Lost Leader* and *The Whiteheaded Boy* as two noteworthy contributions to the English stage.

Boyd, Ernest. *The Contemporary Drama of Ireland.* London: T. Fisher Unwin, Ltd., 1918. This early evaluation of the growth of the Abbey criticizes Robinson's first three plays for their melodramatic tendencies. See pp. 64-69.

———. Introduction to *The Whiteheaded Boy.* Dublin: Talbot Press, Ltd., 1922. Summarizes Robinson's work to date in a more kindly vein.

Bridges-Adams, W. "A National Theatre," *Drama,* No. 51 (Winter, 1958), 27-30. The former director at Stratford-on-Avon calls attention to Robinson's labor of love in fostering the Irish amateur stage to aid the growth of a national drama.

Canfield, Curtis. Introduction, "The Big House." *Plays of the Irish Renaissance.* New York: The Macmillan Company, 1929.

———. Introduction. "Church Street." *Plays of Changing Ireland.* New York: The Macmillan Company, 1936. Both of these anthologies edited by Professor Canfield reflect his sound judgment and good taste.

Chandler, Frank. *Aspects of Modern Drama*. New York: The Macmillan Company, 1939. Refer to the index for discussions of Robinson's early plays.

Clark, B. H. and G. Freedley. *A History of Modern Drama*. New York: Appleton, Century, 1947. Their evaluation of Robinson's plays between 1908 and 1928 puts him in "the respectable rank" of less than the great.

Ellis-Fermor, Una. *The Irish Dramatic Movement*, 2nd ed. London: Methuen and Co., Ltd., 1959. Her book on the evolution of the modern Irish drama is perhaps still the best of its kind.

Fay, Gerald. *The Abbey Theatre*. Dublin: Clonmore and Reynolds Ltd., 1958. The London representative of *The Manchester Guardian* commends Robinson's teamwork with Lady Gregory in keeping the Abbey alive.

Gassner, John. *Masters of Drama*. New York: Dover Publications, 1940. He gives an understanding and balanced appraisal of Robinson's strengths and weaknesses.

Gregory, Lady. *Journals 1916-1930*. Ed. Lennox Robinson. London: Putnam and Co., Ltd., 1946. In abridging these diaries to almost one-quarter of their actual length, Robinson did not delete any of Lady Gregory's unfavorable comments about him.

———. *Our Irish Theatre*. New York: G. P. Putnam's Sons, 1941. She reports fully the Abbey rows in the United States. See pp. 99-101 and 204, among others, for references to Robinson.

Kavanagh, Peter. *The Story of the Abbey Theatre*. New York: Devin-Adair, 1950. His argumentative tone detracts from what is the most stimulating of the histories of the Abbey.

MacLiammoir, Micheál. *All for Hecuba*. London: Methuen and Co. Ltd., 1946. The noted Irish actor in exuberant style gives his impressions of Robinson as director and playwright. Consult the index.

———. *Theatre in Ireland*. Dublin: At the Sign of the Three Candles, 1950.

MacNamara, Brinsley. *Abbey Plays: 1899-1948*. Dublin: At the Sign of the Three Candles, 1949. The succinctness of this survey of the different dramatic trends at the Abbey detracts from its worth. It speaks of Robinson as a leader of trends.

Malone, Andrew E. *The Irish Drama*. New York: Charles Scribner's Sons, 1929. Refers to the index for judicious appraisals of Robinson's contributions to the Irish theatre.

Morgan, A. E. *Tendencies of Modern English Drama*. London: Constable and Co., Ltd., 1924. Traces Robinson's maturing in his plays up to *The Lost Leader*.

Selected Bibliography

Nathan, George J. *The Intimate Notebooks of George Jean Nathan.* New York: Knopf, 1931. He selects Robinson's *The Whiteheaded Boy,* along with three other plays, as samples of the kind of light comedy that Irish and English playwrights write much better than their American counterparts.

Nicoll, Allardyce. *The British Drama.* London: Harrap and Co., Ltd., 1947. Criticizes Robinson for his cynicism in his early plays.

O'Connor, Norreys J. "A Dramatist of Changing Ireland," *Sewanee Review,* XXX (July, 1922), 277-85. Reprinted in his *Changing Ireland.* Cambridge: Harvard University Press, 1924. Discusses Robinson as a writer of short stories and a novel.

Pellizzi, Camillo. *The English Drama.* Trans. Rowan Williams. London: Macmillan and Co., Ltd., 1935.

Philipson, Wulstan Dom. "Lennox Robinson," *The Downside Review,* LXVII (Summer, 1959), 266-70. Comments on Robinson's changing tastes as an editor of poetry anthologies.

Rivoallan, Anatole. *Littérature Irlandaise Contemporaine.* Paris: Hachette, 1939. In chapter six, in examining the Irish theatre since 1916, he credits Robinson for his awareness of the tastes of his audiences.

Robinson, Lennox. (ed.) *The Irish Theatre.* London: Macmillan and Co., Ltd., 1939. Contains the lectures of Andrew E. Malone on "The Rise of the Realistic Movement," pp. 89-116, and of Micheál MacLiammoir on "Problem Plays," pp. 199-227. Each article discusses a different phase of Robinson's work.

Rothenstein, William. *Twenty-Four Portraits.* 2nd Series. London: Chatto and Windus, 1923. Sir William includes a sepia drawing of Robinson in this collection of brief essays on various authors.

Spinner, Kaspar. *Die Alte Dame Sagt: Nein!* Berne: Francke Verlag, 1961. A condensed but scholarly treatment of the dramas of Johnson, O'Casey, and Robinson; places Robinson's plays of middle-class life in the "domestic drama" tradition of Heywood.

Starkie, Walter. "Lennox Robinson: 1886-1958," *The Theatre Annual,* XVI (1959), 7-19. A former fellow director at the Abbey gives a helpful survey of Robinson's different contributions to the Irish theatre.

Trewin, J. C. *The Theatre Since 1900.* London: Andrew Dakers, 1951. He regards *The Lost Leader* as possibly the most original of the new plays on the London stage during 1919.

Weygandt, Cornelius. *Irish Plays and Playwrights.* Boston: Houghton Mifflin Co., 1913. This pioneering work of American scholarship, among the first of the important studies of the Abbey, approves Robinson's hatred of sham and his cleansing satire. Refer to pp. 198-232.

Yeats, William B. *Dramatis Personae.* London: Macmillan and Co.,
Ltd., 1936. Consult pp. 130-32 for Yeats's encouragement of
Robinson for *Cross Roads.*

Index

Carnegie Institute of Technology, 125
Carnegie Library Trust, 77; Central Advisory Committee of, 94, 102, 103
Casement, Sir Roger, 81
Chekhov, Anton, 169
Christianity, Foundations of, 102
Church of Ireland, 29
Cigarette Maker's Romance (Hannan), 42
Civil War, 99, 111-12, 143, 162
Cohen, Dame Harriet, 34
Coleridge, S. T., 159
Collins, Michael, 99
Colonel Newcome (Morton-Thackeray), 41
Colum, Padraic, 39, 40, 43, 44, 57, 58, 62, 163, 164, 168, 173n; *Broken Soil*, 40; *The Land*, 40; *Thomas Muskerry*, 57, 58; *Fiddler's House*, 96
Comedy, 87; in the Irish Theatre, 87-88
Communist China, 161; Government of, 160
Connell, Norreys, 54
Connelly, Marc, 155
Contributions, 34, 40, 42, 43
Cooper, Bryan, 99
Cork, 35, 40, 48; Little Theatre Movement of, 53
Cork Dramatic Society, 52
Corkery, Daniel, 53, 138; *Labour Leader*, 96
Cork Opera House, 36, 40, 42, 43, 130
"Cork Realists," 52
Cork Sportsman, 51
Cornhill, The, 35
Cosgrave, William, 102
Coward, Noel, 103
Coxhead, Elizabeth, 95
Craig, Gordon, 71, 175n
Cummins, Geraldine, 70-71; *Broken Faith*, 70

Dail Eireann, 70
Dante, 78

Davidson, Norris, 108
Davitt, Michael, 35
Deevy, Teresa, 72, 136, 166-67, 179n; *Three Plays*, 179n; Robinson's review of, 179n
Dial, The, 97
Dickens, Charles, 34
Dodd, Lewis, 115
Dolan, Michael, 89
Donovan, Fred, 56
Douglas (Cork), 27
Dowden, Edward, 29, 74, 126
Drama League, Dublin, 100, 112-15 *passim*, 121, 134, 147, 165; British, 102; in United States, 112
Drinkwater, John, 98
Dublin audiences, social traits of, 64
Dublin Castle, 99
Dublin *Evening Telegraph*, 96
Dublin Magazine, 179n
Duke of York Theatre (London), 55
Dunsany, Lord, 70, 97, 104, 114
Dun Theatre (Cork), 52

Easter Week Rebellion, 67, 70, 79, 80
Edward VII, King, death of, 62; funeral of, 63
Edwards, Hilton, 27, 71, 134, 135, 159
Eliott, Gertrude, 41
Ellis-Fermor, Dame Una, 37
Emergency Powers Act, 135
English naturalists, 168
Ervine, St. John, 70, 97, 101
Eton College, 64
Euripides, 114
Evening Telegraph (Dublin), 58
Expressionism, 103, 113-14, 127

Fagan, J. B., 98
Fay brothers, 38, 39, 42
Fays of the Abbey Theatre, 174n
Finlay, Rev. Thomas, 102
Fisherman's Hall (Kinsale), 31, 32
Fitzgerald, Barry, 74, 96, 115
Fitzgerald, Desmond (Senator), 101
Fitzmaurice, George, 47
Florida, 126

London Stage Society, 112
Longford, Lady Christine, 161

Mac Donagh, Donagh, 155
MacLiammoir, Mícheál, 27, 72, 135
MacNamara, Brinsley, 100, 166
MacSwiney, Terence, 98
Mahaffy, Sir John, 29
Manchester Guardian, 63
Markievicz, Countess, 80
Martyn, Edward, 25, 37, 38, 112
Maupassant, Guy de, 134, 136; *Boule de Suif,* 134
Maxine Elliot Theatre (New York), 65
Mayne, Rutherford, 54, 70, 114
Meredith, George, 35
Merriam, Harold G., 125
Mice and Men (Ryley), 41
Michigan, University of, 125
Molesworth Hall, 40
Money Doesn't Matter (Dalton), 153
Montana, University of, (Missoula), 125
Moore, George, 25, 57, 58, 61, 76, 85; *Hail and Farewell,* 57; *Esther Waters,* 57
Moore, Marianne, 97
Moore, Thomas, 74
Munster Fusiliers, 73-74
Murray, T. C., 53, 70, 97, 166; *Birthright,* 61

Nathan, G. J., 169
Nation, The, 35, 42
Nationalism, 30, 35, 36
National Theatre, of Ireland, 101; of England, 102; of Scotland, 102
Naturalism, 61
New York Sun, 65
Nineteenth Century, The, 35
North Carolina, University of, 155
Norwegian Theatre (Bergen), 53

O'Brien, Brendan, 158, 179n
O'Brien, Kate, 26
O'Briens, Dermod The, 77, 78, 88, 94, 139; *see also* Cahirmoyle
Observer, The (London), 101

O'Casey, Mrs. Sean, 101
O'Casey, Sean, 89, 100-101, 143, 168, 169, 176n; *Nannie's Night Out,* 89; *Silver Tassie,* 100; *Plough and the Stars,* 100, 143; *Juno and the Paycock,* 143
O'Connell, Daniel, 35
Oedipus at Colonus, 34
O'Faolain, Sean, 162
O'Higgins, Brian, 99
O'Kelly, Seumas, 70
O'Leary, John, 67, 162
O'Neill-Daunts, The, 35, 42
O'Neill, Eugene, 102, 115, 126, 127; *Emperor Jones,* 127
O'Neill, J. J., 51-52
O'Neill (Allgood) Maire, 42, 51, 56
Only Way, The (Wills-Dickens), 42
Ormonde Dramatic Society, 38, *see also* Fay brothers
Oslo, 155; National Theatre of, 160; *see also* Ring, Gerda
Oxford, 64
Oxford Book of Irish Verse, 155, *see also* Donagh Mac Donagh and Robinson

Parnell, Charles, S., 28, 51, 67, 82, 83, 84
Paymaster General's Office (Dublin), 77
Peacock Theatre, 103, 130
Pearse, Padraic, 80
Pellizzi, Camillo, 169
Pinero, A. W., 154
Pirandello, Luigi, 102, 114, 115, 130; *Henry IV,* 115; *Six Characters in Search of an Author,* 130
Playhouse Theatre (Liverpool), 107
Plunkett, Sir Horace, 77, 78, 81, 94, 179n
Plymouth Theatre (Boston), 65
Provost Trinity College, 102
Purser, Sara, 31, 108

Quinn, John, 66
Quintero, Serafin and Joaquin, 115, 147-48; *The Women Have Their Way,* 148, 178n

Index

Radio Eireann, 34
Realism, Emergence of, 37-40; in Irish theatre, 164
Red Lamp, The (Tristram), 41
Redmond Volunteers, 73
Republican Party, 99, 141
Revolutionist The, 98, *see also* Mac-Swiney
Rice, Mary Spring, 139
Richards, Shelah, 71
Ring, Gerda, 160
Rivoallan, Anatole, 169
Robinson, Lennox, adaptions, 133-36; applied nationalism 77-78; as actor, 115; American influences on, 126-29; appointment to the Abbey, 53-58; "Big House Theme" 138f; cosmopolitanism, 115-24, 165; education 32, 33, 173n; favorite theme, 164; honors, 157f; influence of Yeats on, 66, 67; leader of dramatic trends, 163, 165, 166; "Life in Inish," 149-57; marriage, 125; maturing as producer, 70-73; modern Goldsmith, 169, 170; musical training, 34; nationalist non-dramatic writings, 79-81; organizing librarian for Carnegie Trust, 77f; parents, 28, 29, 30, 31, 54-55; pessimism, 115-24; portraits, 78; producer and lecturer in America, 124-26, 155; relationship with playwrights and actors, 72; religious activities as youth, 32; return to laughter, 147f; romanticism, 163-64; significance of *Church Street,* 129-32; spiritualism, 76; theatrical training in London, 54; theories on playwriting, 67-68; troubled years, 94f; views on producing, 72-73; volunteer in World War I, 73-74

WRITINGS OF:
All's Over Then?, 123-24, 131; Henry Swinnerton, 123-24; Eleanore Swinnerton, 123-24; Maggie, 123-24

The Big House, 139-43, 146, 169, 178n; Kate Alcock, 140-43, 145; Capt. Despard, 140-41; Mr. Alcock, 141-42; Vandaleur O'Neill, 141
Bird's Nest, 151-53, 165; Joseph Fehily, 151-52, 153; Josie 151-152; Hyacinth, 151-52; Stan, 152
Bryan Cooper (biography), 99
Church Street, 112, 126, 129, 132, 136, 138, 149, 166, 178n; Aunt Moll, 131-32; Hugh Riordan, 131-32
The Clancy Name, 43-48; Mrs. Clancy, 44-45, 47; John Clancy, 44-45; Fr. Murphy, 46; Mrs. Spillane, 47, 48
Crabbed Youth and Age (Revolt of the Swans), 103, 108-9, 177n, 178n; Mrs. Swan, 109
Cross Roads, 48-52, 57, 85, 164, 169; Ellen McCarthy, 49, 50, 52, 76, 85, 164; Brian O'Connor, 49, 52; Tom McCarthy, 50
Dark Days (sketches), 80-81; "An Irishwoman," 80; "A Sinn Feiner," 80, 81; "In Silence and Tears," 81;
The Demon Lover, 159-60; Dominic Caughlan, 159-60; Roger Foley, 160; Varina, 160
Drama at Inish (*Is Life Worth Living?*), 138, 149-51, 178n John Twohig, 149-50, 151; Lizzie Twohig, 150; Hector and Constance de la Mare, 150
The Dreamers, 67, 74-76, 88, 126; Robert Emmett, 67, 74-76, 175n; Sarah Curran, 75
Eight Short Stories, 97; "The Chalice," 97, "A Pair of Muddy Shoes," 97
Ever the Twain, 27, 126-28; Carl Svenson, 127-28; Chesterfield Wragsdale, 127-28; Brice Nicholas, 128-29
Far-Off Hills, 137, 138, 147, 149,

159-75 *passim; Oedipus Rex,* 34; *Kathleen ni Houlihan,* 36, 39, 42, 43, 64, 79, 99, 130; *The Hour Glass,* 42, 43; "Hosting of the Sidhe," 42; *The Player Queen,* 96; *At the Hawk's Well,* 100; *Essays,* 109; *Where There is Nothing,* 115

Yonge, Charlotte, 31

Young Farmers' Clubs, 159